All my best,

— Debra Roberts

The
Relationship
Protocol™

How to Talk, Defuse and Build Healthier Relationships

Debra M. Roberts, LCSW
Forward by Joel D. Haber, Ph.D.

Published by JADE oyster

To my husband Jack, for your patience,
kindness, and unwavering love.

Contents

WHAT IS THE RELATIONSHIP PROTOCOL?
- From conflict to communication with the Relationship Protocol
- Do you want stronger, healthier relationships?
- Dr. Freud, this is not therapy or a history lesson
- Looking for the condensed version? That's OK too
- It's simple, not necessarily easy, but worth the effort

HOW DOES THE RELATIONSHIP PROTOCOL WORK?
THE TWO KEY ELEMENTS AND THE FOUR STEPS
- It starts with your commitment
- Shift your thinking because your relationship matters
- The Four Steps: The main ingredients of the Relationship Protocol
- What to expect and when

Foreword
By Dr. Joel Haber

Relationships are transformative; they are the foundation of living in a world with others, and proper communication is essential to making them work. Our joyful and hurtful experiences shape our ideas of intimacy, closeness, and communication, and they determine how we behave in our relationships.

As a clinical psychologist who has worked for more than twenty-five years with thousands of individuals, couples, and families dealing with all types of relationships, I have always wondered why there hasn't been a manual for relationships that provides a *true* template for getting along with others. Where is a road map to guide those who struggle with communication? Is there a "secret sauce" for relationships to help people get along with each other and reduce the mistakes they make time and time again?

A few years ago I reconnected with Debbie Roberts, a friend I have known since we were teenagers. While we were catching up, Debbie described her work as a social worker and her clinical private practice with couples and relationships. She spoke of a model she developed and used in her own practice that helped relationships move forward and get "unstuck." Her success rate with couples was intriguing, and I knew she had developed something special…and unique.

Since Debbie had not discussed her model with anyone besides her clients, she asked if I would evaluate it so we could discuss it further. After learning her method, I realized it was very easy to follow, and it could quickly jump-start positive communication. Debbie had developed a simple, step-by-step guide to help people reconnect and build more effective relationships. This method was different from the relationship/couples models I had been using. Typically, therapists try to work out difficult problems at a time when people are at odds with each other (the reason they seek therapy in the first place). I have found that many of these models can be problematic, because disappointment, anger, and resentment usually get in the way of helping partners work out their negative feelings toward each other.

I decided to test the model with couples and other relationships in my own private practice. It quickly became an effective framework for improving communication between clients who were struggling deeply within their relationships. The results were remarkable. When my clients utilized these tools, I consistently observed transformations and immediate changes in their interactions as well as in their overall relationships. The model became a template for communication that I continue to use today.

The best part is that Debbie has now written a detailed book describing her work, and most significantly, how you can use this technique in your own life. *The Relationship Protocol* is a superb guide for healthy communication and relationship building. It teaches you the fundamental steps to make your relationships thrive. It is an easy-to-understand manual for change with proven results. You will find specific and concrete ways to communicate with the important people in your life as well as how to address problems that affect your relationships. What a gift!

I was thrilled to see how effective *The Relationship Protocol* was in helping my own clients move forward from hurt and disappointment to a more caring place. If you use this protocol and continue to return to it when difficulties arise, you will have the power to transform your relationship into something that can truly flourish. And even more important, this book and its messages are not just for couples. These concepts can be applied to many types of relationships, and you will see instances and examples of that throughout the book. The only impediment to having these tools work would be a lack of openness to using them. It will help you connect in a more positive way and feel closer to the significant people in your life. The Protocol will give you practical strategies to improve your life. It's what you need to build happier and healthier relationships.

I am grateful to Debbie for sharing *The Relationship Protocol* with me, and I am happy she is now able to share it with all of you.

Dr. Joel Haber is a clinical psychologist, author, and internationally recognized anti-bullying speaker and parenting expert who has dedicated more than twenty-five years to the prevention of abusive behaviors in children and adults.

Acknowledgments

While writing this book, I realized that the basic foundation for this method came from my childhood and from hearing how my mother spoke of my father and their relationship. She was a realist; yet she never seemed to get caught up in the little things that typically cause conflicts in relationships. She focused on the big picture—the importance of their relationship—not the problems or the things that tended to get in the way. So thank you, Lila, for your contribution. You and Dad will always be in my heart.

I extend my deepest love and gratitude to my husband and my two children, Eric and Austin. I am thankful every day for our family.

Much appreciation also to the following:

- My brother, Dr. Mark Roberts, my lifelong sounding board, for your honest and intelligent feedback, your unconditional love, and your often humorous point of view.

- Dr. Joel Haber, my dear friend and esteemed colleague, who from the beginning believed in the value of this model and in me. Thank you also for your help in organizing the enormous outpouring of my thoughts.

- Craig O'Keefe, for your encouragement to "just keep writing", your positive energy, quick mind, and boundless creative vision.
- Anne "Grandma" Sperber for squealing with joy at the mere mention of this book.
- My talented colleagues, Kristin Bruning, MD; Keri Chernuchin, PsyD; Seena Russell Axel, PhD; Maureen McKeon, LCSW; Phoebe Kessler, LCSW; Jeanne Crosby, LMHC; and Beverly Wright, LCSW, for your feedback and your friendship.
- My media whiz, Carol Silva, for your "headlines" and your support in this journey.
- Audrey Boyajian, what can I say except, "Long may you run!"
- Sara Montalbano, LCSW, because you always had bigger dreams for me, long before I had them for myself.
- Leo, our sweet, fifty-pound, soft-coated wheaten terrier, who has dutifully been at or on my feet every moment of writing this book.

I send much appreciation and gratitude to my extended family and friends. Thank you for your untiring support and encouragement, as this book became a reality. The positive energy I've received from so many incredible people has humbled and inspired me more than I could ever express.

Finally, I am eternally grateful to all the clients who have come through my door. I thank you for your willingness to be open and your courage to do the work. We've learned from each other, perhaps I more than you.

Introduction

This book is for anyone who wants to communicate better in his or her close relationships, including romantic, family, friendship, and business relationships. I want to give people hope that through healthy communication, all relationships have the potential for change, even in small ways. And personally, my sincere hope is that something about this model connects and resonates with each reader.

―――――――――

When individuals come to me for relationship therapy, understandably, they want to talk about their problems and how unhappy, confused, and perhaps trapped they are feeling. Most of the time, both people arrive together, but many people seek help individually, on their own. They want me to listen and help solve their problems, and many are hoping I can fix or change the other person. Some ask me outright to referee or act as a judge and to pick the winner of their battle. However, the majority of people in therapy simply want and need a safe place to talk about their concerns.

My role is to actively listen and to learn something about the individuals who are seeking help. Initially, I want to know about them: What's going on in their lives? What are their issues and concerns? Why are they seeking treatment now? I may offer some immediate words of support or share some observations. But ultimately, from a relationship perspective, what I'm looking at and what matters most to me is what's going on *between them.* I'm observing *how* they talk to each other, because most of these relationships have one thing in common: They are not communicating well.

This breakdown in communication usually results in both people feeling stuck, unappreciated, or misunderstood. Over time, this disconnect between them generates more problems, such as loneliness, resentment, betrayals, and more. Yet, in my experience, when communication improves, that same relationship has possibilities for change that did not exist before. I have witnessed the transformation of hundreds of relationships, many going from hopeless to hopeful in a short period of time. Showing people how to have healthy relationships and how to communicate effectively empowers them and oftentimes allows even once-stalled relationships to blossom.

I have never thought of myself as a writer. I'm just another therapist, having worked in my private practice for many years. I've always been interested in relationship work, in helping people reconnect, communicate, and defuse conflicts. I've worked with hundreds of struggling couples and many other unhappy or distressed relationships over the years. Through my work, I've learned some important things: there are no quick fixes; and stop looking for fault in others and start looking in the mirror. Ask yourself, "Is there anything else that I can do differently to make this better?" But most important, I've always strongly believed that I cannot help solve the problems in any relationship *unless the individuals can speak to each other in a safe and positive way.* This way of thinking is common sense to me, and it is the driving force behind my work. It's a simple and logical approach to a difficult and often complex problem. I also know that giving people basic communication tools to use outside of our sessions gives them some personal control and confidence, along with a little hope and less vulnerability. The bottom line for me has always been, if people can speak nicely to each other, then maybe we have a shot at building trust and solving their problems.

So, in a very organic way, for the past twenty-five years, I informally developed this communication model around that belief, and I have been teaching it to my clients ever since. Even though my work is based on a therapeutic relationship, the actual method itself is not; it is merely an educational tool. The concepts are basic and practical, and they naturally occur in healthy relationships. In the last twenty-four months, the components have become more organized and put on paper for the very first time. And now the model even has a name: the Relationship Protocol.

I think of the communication between two people as similar to dancing. The energy between the two dancers flows naturally because the movement is graceful and they are both responsive to each other. When they move together, it's fluid and intuitive, because they know each other's next step. If not, they can fall out of sync and even step on each other's toes. Similarly, the "dance" of communication is about positive energy and being responsive to each other.

It's going to take time, effort, and practice on your part for this method to become a more natural and comfortable way of communicating. While reading the book, you also may notice that I repeat things again and again. This is not due to sloppy writing; through repetition I am trying to break a pattern and get you to think differently. Changing *how* someone communicates is not a one-shot deal; it happens over time with a concerted effort and a desire to make a change. To support your efforts, look for *The Relationship Protocol Workbook,* which has exercises to enhance your understanding of the model.

This quote from a client is one of my favorite descriptions of the power of the Relationship Protocol:

> "My relationship sometimes felt like I was driving without holding onto the wheel. Now I know how to steer."

"Whenever I feel overwhelmed and a bit out of control, I remind myself how important this person is to me and how they are a priority in my life. This system taught me to do this."

Chapter One

WHAT IS THE RELATIONSHIP PROTOCOL?

Are you comfortable bringing up sensitive topics? Do you know how to resolve your differences or stop an argument that keeps escalating?

Most people don't. Most people become quiet and ignore the situation, or they get angry and upset, which, of course, never resolves anything. The problems then keep coming back every time the same topic or situation comes up.

Lack of communication and not knowing how to resolve conflicts can create distress and confusion in *any* close relationship.

1

I have been a marital and relationship therapist in private practice for more than twenty years, and I know this statement to be true. Many people in close relationships don't know how to talk to each other. When communication breaks down, conflicts both big and small don't get resolved, and everyone is left feeling unsatisfied.

How we talk to each other is the key.

Problems in relationships don't usually change until the individuals learn how to talk to each other. This means that *the way we communicate* is a critical factor in making our relationships work well.

Everyone wants his or her life to be more enjoyable and less complicated. Yet, as sophisticated as we are, we don't always know how to navigate through the tough times. Because there are no cookie-cutter solutions for solving relationship problems, having some basic communication tools to get through the rough spots can be incredibly helpful.

The Relationship Protocol (also known in this book as "the RP" and "the Protocol") was created just for that purpose. It gives you a framework to help you communicate better in *all* of your important relationships.

Think of the RP like the secret sauce in any great family recipe that makes you want to go back for more. In straightforward terms, the Relationship Protocol will teach you that magic little secret to improving your relationships.

The RP can be used to communicate better or to resolve conflicts with your partner, family members, friends, or business associates.

From conflict to communication with the Relationship Protocol

I frequently work with conflicted relationships that have long histories of problems. Because *how* people argue is far more important than *what* they argue about, I usually start by giving them the RP tools. More often than not, these communication tools help my clients resolve their differences.

Here's the core belief behind the RP model:

> If two people are having problems getting along or their communication isn't great, how can they possibly begin to resolve anything of importance?

I want to teach you how to work through your own issues, build trust in your relationships, and if needed, inject some hope to make things better. You will understand how healthy people communicate and how to defuse and de-escalate conflicts.

Unfortunately, at different times in our lives, we all experience conflicts and relationship struggles. My primary goal is to equip you with new skills to feel more confident and competent in dealing with them.

The RP can teach you how to be a more thoughtful and effective communicator. You will learn how to

- express yourself more comfortably;
- break ongoing negative communication patterns;
- reduce escalating arguments;
- approach the other person and respond more effectively; and
- recover more quickly from conflicts.

Important note: If you are thinking of cutting off a significant person in your life or ending a marriage, consider reading this book first. Learn the RP and make every effort to improve your own communication skills before taking any drastic action. Don't make hasty or impulsive decisions about close relationships.

> Ask yourself this question: When I think of this relationship in the future, will I feel that I made every effort possible to make it better? This is a good reality check before making any big decisions.

If the RP is used consistently, in time you will gain more clarity about yourself and your relationships. If you ultimately decide to end a relationship, you should be able to handle it respectfully and with greater civility after using the RP.

The Relationship Protocol can be your guide for change in all the examples below and many others.

- You may feel unsure about how to make your relationship better.
- You may have a good relationship, but when there's a conflict, emotions fly out of control.
- You may have a difficult or tense relationship, one that makes you feel uncomfortable, unsafe, sad, or lonely.
- You may be afraid that the damage between you and the other person is beyond repair.
- You might have had an argument or conflict, and you're not sure how it started or how to resolve or contain it.
- You may wish you had the words to say when things get uncomfortable between you and the other person.

Learn how to navigate through your close relationships using these tools and strategies, which are proven to work. However, all aspects of the model may not apply to you, so take what you need.

Do you want stronger, healthier relationships?

Relationships are about what happens *between people,* and good communication is the key to a healthy relationship. Research tells us that those individuals who can relate to another person's concerns and who are skilled at defusing arguments have stronger relationships. This means that to have stronger relationships (including romantic, family, friendship, and business) each person

- feels comfortable and safe expressing themselves;
- is not afraid to say how they feel;
- does not feel ignored, cut off, insulted, or afraid to talk;
- knows the other person is listening, because what they say matters;
- understands that building trust and valuing each other is the priority; and
- can count on the other person to resolve issues that are important to the relationship.

Bottom line: Good communication leads to stronger relationships, and you can't solve problems or long-standing issues unless you know *how* to talk to each other. This has to come first before any deeper issues can be changed.

Here are just some of the many scenarios where the Relationship Protocol can help:

- You want to defuse a conversation that is headed in a bad direction.
- Conflicts seem to escalate, and you both say mean or hurtful things in anger or frustration.
- You are not sure how to bring up delicate topics.
- You feel awkward or trapped in your relationship, and it's difficult or even impossible for you to speak or respond in a productive way.
- You keep falling back into familiar negative patterns.

How Change Happens...

As with other goals, such as getting physically fit or developing financial stability, you have to put in the time. You can't magically skip to the last phase. Similarly, changing old communication patterns and habits requires effort and practice. Eventually, the new skills become your "new normal" as the model is integrated into your life. The three phases of the RP are learn, practice, and integrate.

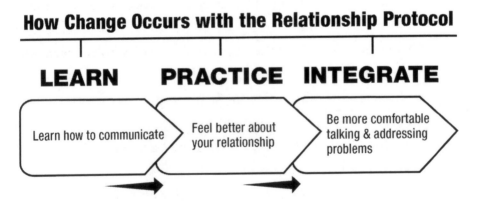

How Change Occurs with the Relationship Protocol

LEARN   **PRACTICE**   **INTEGRATE**

Learn how to communicate   Feel better about your relationship   Be more comfortable talking & addressing problems

Think about it: When you are immersed or stuck in your relationship problems, it can seem almost impossible to work together to resolve issues. By learning the model and using it on a consistent basis, you'll gain new skills to help you tackle some of the issues that were otherwise off the table.

Here's how the process works:

1. **Learn:** In the beginning, when you are unfamiliar with the model, you can still affect change, as long as you are making an effort. As you start using the RP, you may notice some change relatively quickly, either within yourself or in the other person. Perhaps you are noticing more self-awareness on your part, some positive communication between you and the other person, or a different kind of connection. In troubled relationships, this is where the ray of hope comes into play early on.

2. **Practice:** The more you consistently practice using the model, the more comfortable you will become at communicating. Hopefully you will have positive experiences, which will set the stage for trust to be built.

3. **Integrate:** In time, communication feels more natural and comfortable. You now have more confidence in each other and stronger communication skills to delve into issues and problems.

Got kids?

Learning how to communicate better affects everyone in your household. If there is always negativity or tension, or if you are bickering or fighting in front of your children, *you are affecting them.* If they are uncomfortable or fearful in their home, you may be changing their view of themselves and of the world. Ongoing fighting or strained relationships can result in children feeling angry, scared, insecure, confused, self-hatred, and more. They may become hypervigilant, paying close attention to what's going on and noticing their parents' interactions. They may also avoid spending time at home or in your company if doing so makes them unhappy.

As an adult, you are their role model of how to behave with others. Unfortunately, what you do and say on a regular basis may well become their "inheritance" for communication in their future relationships. Remember: If you have children and you are in a difficult relationship, they are one of your motivations for learning and using the RP. Don't be discouraged. It's never too late to model healthy communication and change your legacy.

Good communication can change your perspective

The RP mimics the tenets of healthy relationships. It shows you how to function as if you are communicating in a healthy relationship. In a relatively short amount of time, the model can transform the way you communicate in all your close relationships.

Underlying problems are often rooted in poor communication and mistrust.

A large percentage of people found that after using the RP, many of the relationship problems that existed before were no longer problems.

Bottom line: When people start feeling more comfortable together and relating differently to each other, everything between them can change. You will gain a new skill set. These tools can impact how you relate to each other and may change your perspective on your relationship.

Dr. Freud, this is not therapy or a history lesson

The Relationship Protocol is a communication tool. It is an educational program, not a therapeutic technique.

The primary focus of psychotherapy is to better understand the "whys" of your thinking and/or the "whys" of your behavior. Therapy is about introspection and personal growth. By contrast, the RP teaches people how to talk to each other *today*. If along the way you figure out the "whys," that's a wonderful bonus.

This model also stays focused in the present, not the past. It gives you the tools you need to talk to each other today, in real time, in a positive and constructive manner. Because the RP doesn't address your problems, history, or emotions, no one has to feel emotionally exposed or too vulnerable. It gets right to the point of learning to communicate first.

This method even allows tough relationships to have a fresh start. For example:

- A couple barely speaks to one another about anything important without fighting.
  - ❑ How can we expect them to realistically figure out their problems together?

- Two people have a good relationship. They rarely argue, but when they do, it's about small, trivial things that quickly spiral out of control.
  - ❏ How can they speak differently, prevent blowing things out of proportion, and reduce the escalating fights?
- A supervisor at the office doesn't return phone calls, and there's a deadline requiring information from him.
  - ❏ How can you approach him without angering him to get the necessary information?
- Parents are concerned that their daughter is shutting down, not communicating, and seems depressed.
  - ❏ How can they address their concerns without getting frustrated or angry?
- A grandmother is feeling sad because she hasn't seen her grandchildren in a long time. She knows they've been very busy but hesitates to mention her feelings to her son for fear of sounding critical.
  - ❏ How can she speak to her son so he doesn't hear her feelings as judgmental?

These examples only scratch the surface. The Relationship Protocol can show you how to speak with others on a daily basis, not just when there's a problem.

Looking for the condensed version? That's OK too

If you aren't interested in reading a self-help book from cover to cover, you can find the core ideas in one place in chapter 2.

The entire Relationship Protocol model is there, along with a brief description of each of the components. Throughout the book, I have highlighted important points and tips. Additionally, at the end of chapter 16, you will find a basic outline of the Relationship Protocol model.

You can't get a full understanding of how the model's Key Elements and the steps work together without reading the whole book. You won't absorb how to deal with the ups and downs, stressors, and common stumbling blocks. Readers of the entire book will see that the RP is a comprehensive communication guide, one they can always come back to whenever they hit rocky patches. Yet, if that's not your thing, then check out the shortcuts.

Leave your bad attitude at the door

Many people approach new things with a negative slant—a "prove it to me" attitude. They look through a microscopic lens to find flaws, negatives, and justifiable reasons for failure. This attitude is a setup for disappointment, and like most things, the Relationship Protocol will not work if this is how you approach it. The RP is also not about blaming others or waiting for someone else to change, because you cannot control what anyone else chooses to do.

If you want your relationship to be better, you have to commit to an "I want this to work" attitude. Make a conscious decision to believe in this model because it has a proven track record and/ or because of your personal desire to have better relationships.

Your need for a positive mind-set can't be emphasized enough. Just showing up isn't enough. You have to be an active, ongoing, and willing participant.

It's simple, not necessarily easy, but worth the effort

Changing old patterns and habits requires time and patience. Transforming your communication habits slowly can reduce expectations and disappointments if things don't move along as you hoped or anticipated. Think of it as a building process; we learn to walk by placing one foot in front of the other, and then we learn to run. The same is true here.

If you invest some time and add a touch of motivation, you will have a much greater chance at improvement.

The RP will work if you commit to begin using it right now. Decide to be accountable to yourself and your relationship, and decide that you want to become a better partner, family member, or friend.

Consider using this book as an ongoing reference guide—an encyclopedia of sorts—and stick with the model, whether progress reveals itself or not. These are lifelong tools for you, regardless of how others respond.

Eventually this model can become the new normal for how you relate in all of your important relationships.

Think of the kinds of relationships that you would like to have in your life.

As you read through the book, choose a close relationship that you would like to work on, such as one with your spouse, fiancé, girlfriend, boyfriend, life partner, friend, significant other, parent, in-law, sibling, family member, colleague, business partner... You get the point. This book is designed to help you communicate better in all of those relationships.

(Names when used have been changed to protect the privacy of the individuals and some examples are compilations of more than one relationship.)

Now let's get going...

Dr. Martin Luther King said, "Take the first step in faith. You don't have to see the whole staircase, just take the first step."

It's your turn. Take that first step, and let change start with you!

"This model basically took a lit stick of dynamite and cut the fuse. We were in bad shape, but using the RP, things have turned around. It takes work, but it's worth it."

Chapter Two

HOW DOES THE RELATIONSHIP PROTOCOL WORK? THE TWO KEY ELEMENTS AND THE FOUR STEPS

Two Key Elements are the basis for positive communication. They set the stage for a healthier relationship and lay the solid foundation for the Four Steps.

Think of your relationships in terms of these two Key Elements, and let this begin to shift your thinking in a more open and positive direction.

It starts with your commitment

Key Element #1: *Commitment*

The first Key Element asks you to commit to making an effort to better your relationship.

"I want to work on this relationship and make it better."

If you sincerely believe these words, this method will show you how to work on your relationship and improve it. Your commitment can also infuse some hope for change, particularly if your relationship is strained.

"Commitment" may sound simple, but it is essential to moving toward a new way of behaving in your relationship. If you are willing to make that effort and *commit to the process* by becoming more positive and open, it will provide the fuel for change.

Commitment is required to be successful.

Remember: A commitment means stick-to-itiveness—staying with the program regardless of challenges or setbacks. Commitment is a *mandatory* element, and quite frankly, it's the only way things can really change.

To be successful, commitment is required. Unless you're willing to commit to the process, don't expect any significant results. Those who don't commit will generally not stick around when conflicts or difficult issues arise. No commitment means no success, and this Key Element is required for success.

Here's why:

This is the first conscious decision you are making toward changing your relationship. Because you can control only yourself and your own decisions, change begins with you. Ask yourself, "Who do I want to be in this relationship?" Can you commit to making the effort to be that person?

You are also committing to the process, not necessarily the person.

If you are in a difficult relationship and unsure of your future or your commitment to the person, there is no pressure here to make that type of commitment. Key Element #1 is the commitment to making an effort to better your relationship. It is not necessarily a commitment to the person, but to *the process of learning and using the model.* In the end, by using the Relationship Protocol (hopefully together), you may gain more clarity about your feelings and your relationship.

Relationships are unpredictable, and you will be tested. Every relationship encounters tough spots and has moments, reactions, tensions, and external challenges that you cannot control. You will have difficult, challenging, miserable moments when you will be asked to call upon your commitment to the process (Key Element #1) and your stick-to-itiveness. During those times, giving up will not be an option, because you are now involved in and committed to the process with new tools to help you.

Shift your thinking because your relationship matters

Key Element #2: *Shift Your Thinking*

Next, let's look at your thinking and your perceptions about your relationship.

Most of the time when there's a problem, a rough patch, or a conflict, you may focus on what's missing. Even worse, you may zoom in and focus on what's wrong with the other person and/or your situation. That negative zoom lens will always remind you of the other person's flaws or the weaknesses in the relationship. In that moment, you don't want to be close to them; who would? In essence, you are turned off and turned away from them. When you're turned away, you can disregard them. You may not be as interested in them or concerned about hurting their feelings. This lack of connection can be toxic, and it can continue for however long the turning-away thinking occurs.

Sometimes these negative feelings can build over time, but turning away can also happen quickly, particularly when you are embroiled in an argument with someone close to you. You might blurt out insults or say something that hurts them deeply because you know their hot buttons.

In general, if you are turned away, you are also usually tuned out and more apt to say hurtful things. Can you relate to this familiar refrain: "Who cares about them and what they think!" Most of us have said something like this at one time or another. When this disconnect is happening, you are probably more interested in blaming, staying annoyed, and complaining, rather than having a reasonable resolution. In that moment, you have lost sight of the importance of this person and their value to you.

Look at it this way: When you stop appreciating them, you stop paying attention. You can lose interest in what they have to say and how they feel. You may even behave as if they simply don't matter.

Keeping the second Key Element in mind, you would instead, metaphorically, turn toward them. You must switch your thinking from what is missing and what is wrong with them and/or the relationship and refocus on their importance to you and your desire to make the relationship better. Through the anger, hurt, and sadness, there is still an understanding that this person and this relationship are important to you.

Key Element #2 asks you to begin thinking with a new perspective.

"This is someone who is important to me, and I want to get along better with them. I am going to stop looking at the past problems and stop focusing on the negatives about our relationship. I am going to try to improve things going forward, even when times are tough."

If you do this, you have begun the process of shifting your thinking. In that moment, you let the importance of the relationship become your primary focus.

The gist of the message is, change your energy and your thinking to focus on the importance of this person and this relationship today, whatever that means to you.

Key Element #2 asks you to put your relationship before the issue and before the problems in your past.

Important note: The Relationship Protocol model doesn't negate the past, but for now, the focus is on changing how you speak to each other *today* and how you think about the relationship and the other person.

That means you must stop disconnecting and begin the process of turning toward the other person; focus on appreciating them in the present, even when times are tough. This can happen only if you have a true desire to make things better and you are committed to the process (Key Element #1).

For today, focus on communicating with and appreciating this person.

Problems are put aside for now. The issues will be there; they are not going away. In the beginning, the primary goal is to learn how to communicate with each other before addressing any of the issues between you.

Essentially, you want to move forward more than you want to focus on your anger or frustration.

This shift changes your attitude from a singular "me" or "I" focus to a relationship "us" and "we" focus. **Look inward and ask yourself, "How can I be the best person, friend, colleague, or family member to this person who is important to me?"** This introspection puts the ball in your court. You can only control what you do and how you think. Stop trying to change them; instead shift your thinking and choose to appreciate them.

Depending on your situation, this shift can be subtle or dramatic. Either way, it will make a difference. It's also a great way to start using the Relationship Protocol!

This is the first big step toward making things better, because you are actively putting the relationship first and, if necessary, your negative history behind you.

Turning toward the other person can change everything. So turn the dial just a little bit and dare to change your energy and your thinking, simply because the other person matters to you.

The two Key Elements ask each of you, as committed individuals in this process (Key Element #1), to make a decision to turn toward the other person and shift your thinking (Key Element #2). For many, this will be a perspective change and will require you to think differently. Let the Key Elements serve as a prompt for how to best communicate and think about the important people in your life. In time and with practice, this new outlook will feel more instinctive and natural.

Do you have the Key Elements now?

If the Key Elements already happen naturally in your relationship, that's great! You have the foundation in place for building positive communication using the Relationship Protocol. Your relationship has a healthy framework; you may just need to plug in some communication tools.

Examples of applying the two Key Elements

Your spouse has repeatedly said that she doesn't feel appreciated by you. You're stunned at how she feels, because in your mind, she's wrong; you do appreciate her.

Let's apply the Key Elements: If you are committed to making this relationship better (Key Element #1) and you value your partner (Key Element #2), you don't want her to feel unappreciated. Even if you think this is an unbelievable or ridiculous feeling on her part, stay with the direction of the Relationship Protocol. You don't want her to feel that way because you are committed to the relationship (Key Element #1) and you care about her feelings (Key Element #2). If you react defensively or get upset, this will exacerbate the situation and won't change anything, including her feelings. Ignoring her comments or not addressing them may also set you back, and it might stop her from being open with you in the future.

In this situation, even if your wife is wrong (because you do appreciate her) or you are surprised or confused about her feelings, it is your responsibility to shift your thinking and let her know that she is appreciated. Instead of focusing on how frustrating it is that she doesn't feel appreciated, stop and think, "How can I let her know that I do appreciate her?" Don't get defensive or annoyed, but address her comments with genuine concern and interest because her feelings matter to you.

It's important for both people to feel good in your relationship. You can ask your wife directly what you can do to make things better. And if she is truly important to you, why doesn't she know this? What do *you* need to do differently? Make an effort to keep the second Key Element in mind when you think of your relationship.

You have an argument with your best friend about something that is important to both of you. You're upset and very unhappy, and you are not ready to talk about the problem.

Instead of never speaking again or saying hurtful things to or about each other, your goal is to somehow let your friend know she is important to you, even though you are upset. It can be something small, such as a smile or saying "hello" when you're in each other's company. You could reach out and tell the person, "I'm still upset. I'm just not ready to talk" or "You're still important to me, but I need some time." Anything, even a few words, is better than ignoring or escalating an already tough situation.

When you acknowledge that you are not ready to talk about the issue but that your friend is still important to you, you are applying the two Key Elements. You are committing to the process of improving the relationship (Key Element #1), and you are letting the person know you still value them, even through this rough patch (Key Element #2).

One of your largest customers can be difficult at times. Yet regardless of your feelings, you need to keep the relationship with him on good terms.

You find yourself avoiding his calls because you don't want to deal with his complaints or his unreasonable demands.

If this customer is important to your business, your primary role is to shift your thinking (Key Element #2); change your energy and your focus. This is someone who should be appreciated as a valued customer, not thought of as an annoying person. Think about the importance of the relationship between you and how you represent yourself or your company when you avoid his calls.

Be professional and friendly; change how you view this customer by respecting his opinions and listening to his complaints as well as his demands. Think of it this way: instead of looking at what is wrong and how difficult he is, remind yourself that this customer is important to your company. For this reason alone, you want him to feel respected and appreciated in order to maintain your good standing (both Key Elements).

Another set of problems occurs if he is abusive or making ridiculous demands. But in this example and in general, it's a simple turn of the dial to change your perspective in a more positive direction, if only for the sake of your business.

You frequently argue with your ex-husband. He's not a bad person, but it's always been a tense and strained relationship, especially around issues relating to the shared custody of your children. You feel overwhelmed and trapped in this longstanding stressful situation, and you worry about the emotional effect it is or will have on your children.

This is a common challenge for many families. For the sake of your children and to also decrease the stress level in your own life, it is important for you to make a conscious decision to shift your thinking about your ex-husband. If you can change your perspective from seeing him as "the enemy" to a sincere desire to get along better, simply because of the role he plays in your children's lives, this new way of thinking will influence how you interact with and relate to him.

When you take control of who *you* want to be in your relationship with your ex-husband, you will probably feel less vulnerable and your feelings of being overwhelmed and trapped may be greatly reduced. However, regardless of how he continues to interact with you, make an effort to stay focused on what's important: the well being of your children and keeping your life less burdened. And when you refuse to argue, but instead remain calm and respectful, you are changing the direction of that one interaction. These positive interactions can then build on each other and grow. Use the Relationship Protocol model to give you the language you need to be more thoughtful, to reduce escalations, and to defuse conflicts in challenging relationships.

Here they are again

The Key Elements ask you to think about your relationship from a healthier place. They affect how you look at the relationship, which directly impacts how you approach and respond to the other person.

Key Element #1: A commitment to making an effort to better your relationship by promising to stick with the process even during the negative times.

Key Element #2: Shift your thinking. Turn toward the other person, value them, and think about the relationship today. How do you want them to feel in this relationship? Change from a "me" or "I" focus to an "us" focus, and put the relationship first, before the past or any issues between you.

Let's review the Relationship Protocol essentials:

The two Key Elements are the foundation of the Relationship Protocol model. They are always in play, even during challenging times, as a constant reminder of your commitment to the process and your concern for the other person. They fine-tune your thinking and shift your perspective by bringing the relationship focus to the forefront of your mind.

Reread this section if you don't yet understand the Key Elements. Be patient. In time it will begin to make sense and gel.

The Four Steps: The main ingredients of the Relationship Protocol

The Four Steps are more action-oriented than the two Key Elements are. They are your tools for how to communicate in a more positive and helpful way.

The steps establish your commitment to change and your willingness to work on your relationship.

You don't have to memorize the steps now, but the more time and effort you take to learn, understand, and use them, the sooner you will see change. They are repeated many times throughout the book. Before long, you will see why each step is important and how they are related.

Each step will be explained later in much more detail. For now, just remember they work in concert with the two Key Elements.

These words show your commitment

Step #1: "I want to get along with you."

"I want to be closer to you."

If there are conflicts, add, "I don't want to fight with you."

Step #2: "I am going to be kind. I am not going to be mean or sarcastic."

Step #3: "I am never going to do anything to intentionally hurt you." (Add "from now on" if you have done hurtful things in the past.)

Step #4: "I am going to give you the benefit of the doubt."

The steps are a critical component for success. They are active tools to help you

- communicate more effectively;
- defuse and de-escalate heated emotions during conflicts; and
- provide a framework for healthier and more satisfying relationships.

There is no right or wrong way to begin using the Four Steps, and some steps may apply to you more than others. You can begin working with them in a number of ways, whichever is most comfortable for you. Think about the following options.

If you are working with another person to improve your relationship:

- Acknowledge to the other person and to yourself that you are committed to improving your relationship.
- State the commitment out loud to each other.
- After reviewing the model, show it to the other person and give them a copy of the Relationship Protocol outline in chapter 16.
- To make a stronger statement and stronger commitment to the process, both of you can sign the bottom of the printed page as a contract between you.
- Learn the mantra in chapter 8, because it is a condensed version of the Relationship Protocol.

If you are making an effort on your own to improve your communication skills or a specific relationship:

- Acknowledge your personal commitment to yourself. This personal acknowledgment emphasizes the conscious decision you are making to become a better communicator.
- Read the Key Elements and Four Steps. Print out the Relationship Protocol model and mantra in chapter 16.
- Learn the mantra.
- One person can make a significant impact when they bring positive change to any relationship. Stay with it!

What to expect and when

The length of time it takes to see results will vary for each relationship. It generally takes thirty days to break a habit. So consider that time frame as your starting point for changing patterns of behavior and communication. Some pertinent factors include, but are not limited to

- how motivated and willing one or both of you are to make the effort;
- each person's level of self-awareness, emotional health, and communication skills;
- how healthy or damaged the relationship is;
- the ability and willingness of one or both parties to follow the model on a consistent and committed basis; and/or
- each individual's readiness to participate and not sabotage the progress by being negative, angry, or dishonest, or trying to prove the model wrong.

In the beginning, if you make an effort to change how you communicate based on the tenets of this model, you may notice changes within days. You can't fully trust these changes yet, but even small changes show you that change is possible. That's motivating.

If you continue to use the RP tools and focus *every day* on being the best communicator you can be, change begins to take root. Within weeks, you and the other person may experience a significant difference in the way you relate to each other. Within months, the behavior may begin to feel like the new normal, and you will have more natural, healthier relationships.

A few things to consider

Your words should reflect your pure intentions and feelings about getting along better. The model works only because the effort you put forth is genuine.

However, if you are intentionally dishonest or insincere, just going through the motions, not interested in bettering the relationship, and full of empty apologies, you may as well stop now. Please don't waste anyone's time, because your insincerity will only cause more conflict and pain all around. This is your opportunity for change. Can you make an effort to be thoughtful, respectful, and honest?

Don't set your expectations too high in the beginning. It will take time to understand the model, learn the RP, and use it effectively.

And when you make mistakes, you may get discouraged, but there are no judgments here. Give yourself credit for trying, and remember your sense of humor, because it will come in handy. When you and/or they mess up, always go back to the two Key Elements: your commitment to making an effort, and focusing on your relationship and appreciating each other. This will get you back on track. Be willing to learn from each slip-up, and use the language of the steps as your guide.

Most close relationships eventually have to learn how to deal with some conflict.

Healthy relationships have plenty of conflicts, and the people in them make mistakes too; it's just a part of life for all of us. However, when you begin to trust each other's intentions (Step #3) and learn how to recover, everything can change for the better!

A real-life example of the Relationship Protocol in action: From almost-divorced to healthy communication

A couple decided to attend marital therapy. The wife was unhappy and ready to get divorced. She had already met with a lawyer and was a step away from leaving. Her husband finally agreed to go for therapy, but by then she was clearly not interested. She was neither hopeful nor optimistic about their future, even though her husband was now saying he was willing to work on their relationship. She had basically checked out of the marriage.

After meeting with me a few times, they both agreed to give the RP a try. The husband liked having the model as a reference guide. The wife thought it all seemed too fake or scripted. I encouraged her to give it some effort, but she had a "not until you prove it to me" attitude. Over the next few weeks, the wife gradually noticed that her "typically uncommunicative and distant husband" was now speaking kindly to her, making a distinct effort to change. He made small gestures that she noticed and appreciated. He had also shown his commitment to follow the model, regardless of his wife's hesitation. He reported finding it easy to do so, and he always kept a copy of the model on hand.

The wife was amazed that her husband could make any change at all. She became more willing to try the model after witnessing the small behavioral changes in him, and soon she made a conscious decision to also follow the RP. Within a few weeks, they both became somewhat hopeful about their relationship—for the first time in more than fifteen years.

Each week they continued to report a calmer and more cooperative household. Both were pleased with their progress and surprised at how quickly and easily things turned around with the tools from the RP. After a while, the husband was still content with the way things were going, but the wife became impatient with the process and wanted to fix all of the things that were wrong in their relationship. Because they both reported feeling better about their communication, I encouraged them to begin slowly addressing some of their issues, using the RP as their guide.

A few months later, the wife reported how amazed she was that they were still going strong. She said they would often remind each other to use the RP, and they even had a few discussions—which previously would have ended in explosions—that did not go badly at all. Instead they were no big deal. The wife felt they appreciated each other more, and because of this, they had fewer arguments. They came to understand that each time one of them made an effort to communicate with the other, they were not trying to hurt anyone's feelings or be right. Things were easier between them, and they both noticed a positive difference and could more easily share how they felt.

I told them they were now using the RP model more naturally. The wife was confused, stating that she really liked the RP, but in her mind, they had used the model only in the beginning, when they needed to learn communication tools. I reminded them that the components of the model are based on how healthy relationships function. After using the model for a while, it becomes the natural way to communicate and relate in a healthier and more positive way.

They were pleasantly surprised and happy at how far they had come within a few months of learning the RP, and they were pleased at how it had changed their perspective on their relationship and their lives. I reminded them that it's not uncommon to slip back into their old ways, and I encouraged them never to get casual about how they communicate with each other.

This kind of positive outcome has happened hundreds of times in my office. And this is my goal for you: that you also experience happier, healthier, and more positive relationships.

"When I use the steps, it softens everything for me.
The whole situation gets a little easier."

Chapter Three

WHAT IF ONLY ONE PERSON PARTICIPATES?

Frequently only one person in a relationship uses the Relationship Protocol. One person can make a significant difference in changing communication, and it can be a personally gratifying and eye-opening experience.

Learn the RP for yourself. Whether you're curious enough to read this book or want to refine your own communication skills or choose to work on your relationship without the other person getting involved, you can create change. If you open your mind and your heart to those around you, you automatically expand your world.

For those situations where the other person isn't interested in learning the model, please don't interpret their behavior harshly. Instead of focusing on why they don't want to use it or what they are not doing, use the RP to better understand yourself and, by default, your relationship. If you change how you communicate, things will change between and for you and them. You may even gain some clarity about your relationship, the other person, and most certainly about yourself.

Trust the other person's intentions.

Give the other person the benefit of the doubt (Step #4) that their intentions are not to hurt you (Step #3). This may be all they have to offer you for now. If you begin by trusting their intentions, it will change how you view them and how you relate to them. Let the changes with the RP model start with you. In time, the other person may notice the positive changes you are bringing to the relationship, and that may inspire them to give it a try.

Changing the cycle of communication

Relationships are similar to the gears on a clock that all work together. Each mechanism is connected in some way. When one gear moves, the others move. If one gear slows down, the rest of the gears slow down. People in close relationships affect each other similarly in both positive and negative ways.

For example, if you change your behavior by deciding to be kind and not engage in arguing, you immediately change the energy between you and the other person. They are forced to respond differently to you because you are not repeating your expected communication pattern. It takes two people to argue. If you choose not to participate or if you respond in a more positive manner, you have successfully changed the course of that one interaction. Each interaction then builds on the next. This is how one person affects change in their relationships.

You can make this choice right now: commit to the process, start behaving differently, and don't engage in negative interactions.

The "Gears of a Clock" diagram illustrates how close relationships are interconnected and affected by each other.

Gears of a Clock

Depending on your circumstances, there can be limitations to the extent or duration of the changes. But do it for yourself—without hesitation! It's empowering to know that you can make a difference in your life, whether or not others participate with you.

"When he says 'Step 1' to me, it immediately diffuses the situation."

Chapter Four

STEP #1: "I WANT TO GET ALONG WITH YOU."

Step #1 in plain English:

"I want to get along with you."

"I want to be closer to you."

If there are conflicts, add, "I don't want to fight with you."

When you say these or similar words to another person, you are telling them that you are ready for a positive change in your relationship. You are stating that you want things to be better and you want to get along better. You are reassuring them that you want this relationship to work, or at the very least, you want it to work better than it has in the past.

This commitment is really big and extremely important. You are essentially telling the other person, "I am changing from focusing on me to paying more attention to our relationship. If there are conflicts, I am going to try to change from focusing on my unhappiness to valuing you and our relationship."

Step #1 may sound basic and too elementary to be effective, but don't underestimate the power and impact of these few words. You don't have to use all of them or recite them word for word if they feel too scripted; it's the idea behind them that you should express.

When to use Step #1:

- **To reassure the other person**
- **When you are uncertain as to what to say**
- **During times of conflict or potential conflict**

You can use the statements together or alone, according to whatever fits your relationship. Here are examples of what you might say:

- "I want to get along with you."
- "I don't want to fight with you."
- "I want us to be closer."
- "I want to get along with you. I really don't want to fight. Let's try to be nicer to each other."
- "Let's stop arguing and try to approach this differently. I want to get along, be closer, and not fight."
- "I'm not sure how to make things better, but I want to get along better and be closer."

- You can always add "I think you also want things to be better."

When you change your approach and say sincere, positive statements like these, you immediately change the energy between you and the other person from negative to positive. You are injecting something different and positive, which quickly reminds both of you about wanting to get along, focusing on the relationship, and liking each other. You are also telling them that the relationship is important to you.

You can defuse conflict

When one or more of the Step #1 statements is verbalized, you can quickly disarm the other person's anger and negativity. This may lead to something unexpected, because they may begin making an effort as well. When you say with sincerity any or all of the statements in Step #1—"I want to get along with you," "I want to be closer to you," and/or "I don't want to fight with you"— the negative energy cycle between you and the other person can quickly shift to a more positive one. Most likely, they haven't heard this before, so when you say you want a positive change in a way that they can believe, great things can happen.

Warning: If the other person doesn't react positively at first, don't be surprised or discouraged, because this is a building process. Hang in there and stay with it!

The power of the pause button

What if you have a disagreement or a conflict and you're both upset with no clue about how to stop or resolve it? It may seem like

41

everything you say to each other is making the situation worse and escalating the argument. This negative cycle can stump both of you and can even occur sometimes around minor issues. Using the Relationship Protocol, here's what you can do:

> Simply stop talking for a moment and hit the pause button. Then take a breath, and sincerely speak from your heart about your desire to make things better. Say one, two, or all of the sentences of Step #1, whichever are applicable. If you can, speak in a calm, neutral tone, because how you approach the conversation can affect the outcome.

Step #1 has the power to change the direction of a negative situation.

You can immediately stop the action between you and the other person and defuse a potentially escalating fight or one that has already spiraled out of control. Think of Step #1 as a quick, self-imposed intervention. It is one of the best and simplest ways to change the direction of a mounting conflict. Hit the pause button and then calmly and thoughtfully say something about your desire to get along and not fight in that moment. Essentially, if you refuse to fight, the fight can't continue.

Step #1 also moves you toward the ultimate goal of building trust.

During times of conflict, your positive comments can help you both see that the negative back-and-forth is toxic and needs to stop immediately.

Whenever you are unsure of what to say in a critical moment, use Step #1 as your script, and then collect your thoughts before continuing. All of the Relationship Protocol's steps offer some options for handling these difficult situations.

A Heated Argument Gets Neutralized with Step #1: When Love Is a Battlefield

Steven reported that he very angrily stormed out of the room because he was so enraged at his wife, Lauren, during an argument and was ready to explode. In the next moment, he thought about the relationship and the Relationship Protocol. He took a deep breath, turned around, and went back into the room. Because this was the first time he was using the steps, he said to Lauren, "I'm still really angry at you, and I'm really not sure what else I'm supposed to say, but I really do want to get along with you, and I don't want us to fight." He got control of his anger and used the RP script he had just learned to help disarm his emotions in that moment.

Lauren reported feeling impressed that her husband had remembered to use Step #1. She admitted to completely forgetting about the model in the heat of their argument, although she was very happy that Steven had remembered. She observed that even though he was upset with her, he was able to put aside his anger to stop the argument and make their relationship the priority (the essence of Key Element #2).

In this example, the husband's sincere act immediately stopped the escalation and the expression of anger between the couple. They were both able to let go of the fight and remember that their relationship was more important than whatever issue they were fighting about. It didn't matter who was right or wrong. Steven placed the relationship before the specific issue, which had an enhanced benefit. His partner appreciated the gesture and the sentiment. It showed effort, desire for change, and caring. It also showed them a strategy to stop the angry words that had hurt both of them so many times in the past.

The Lesson: In the throes of a conflict, you can still take control and change the trajectory with just a few meaningful words. After a disagreement occurs, take a few minutes to collect your thoughts. Then go back to the other person and talk to them about the importance of the relationship to you (turn toward them and show them that you value them). Explain that they are your priority, even though you may still be upset. Remember to use the language of Step #1 if you are uncertain of the words to say.

An Inexperienced Communicator Uses Step #1: "I Really Like You"

A shy man in his thirties with limited communication skills sought help for his relationship with Brooke, his new girlfriend. He was concerned that his poor communication skills would lead to an end to their relationship. It was suggested that he use Step #1:"Tell your girlfriend simply, but honestly, that she is important to you and that you want to get along better and be closer to her."

He reported back that when he said those words (Step #1), Brooke told him she felt that he truly cared. The Relationship

Protocol gave him the language to let his girlfriend know that she mattered to him, and this reassured her of his feelings. He reported feeling a boost of confidence because this was the first time he had talked about his intimate feelings with someone he cared about.

Summary: When you are struggling with what to say during a confusing or difficult time, remember to first hit the pause button, then take a moment and simply say one or all of the statement(s) in Step #1:

- "I want to get along with you."
- "I want to be closer to you."
- If appropriate, add "I don't want to fight with you."

These simple words (or your own words, if they are similar in intent) will help change stuck or angry feelings and will move the two of you toward a more positive connection.

Here's why this works:

Your focus immediately changes from an "I" conflict and problem focus to valuing "us" messaging (Key Elements). When your focus is on "us" and the relationship, it is not about doing it right or winning the point of the argument. In healthy communication, the "us" messaging reminds both of you that the relationship is not a competition; it needs to be protected, not destroyed.

This "us" messaging also gives the other person a chance to respond in kind. However, regardless of their reaction, stay on point and continue to put forth effort, even if they don't respond as you hope they would. This is where your commitment to the process comes into play. Give it time and stick with it (Key Element #1), because time will prove that you are sincere, that the relationship is important to you (Key Element #2), and that you want to get along (Step #1). You may have to show the other person how serious you are before they come around.

Friend Example Using Step #1: "What the Heck Is Going On?"

The example below could take place with a friend or any other important relationship in any number of situations. The main premise is that you notice your friend seems to be upset with you. It may happen while on the phone, out to dinner, texting, playing cards, at work, or in just about any situation.

Using the Relationship Protocol, your goal is to use Step #1 language as your script when you're unsure how to approach a topic.

During a weekly pickup basketball game, your friend is playing with much more aggression than usual. He seems irritated and is intentionally fouling you and making rude comments about you under his breath. You ignore his behavior and try to concentrate on playing the game.

This is a situation where you have to wait until the game ends before approaching your friend. Talking about his behavior while you're on the court could result in an explosion of emotions at an inappropriate time, and that wouldn't resolve anything. You can wait until the game is over or until the next day when you have an opportunity to talk and can speak calmly using Step #1.

When you initiate the conversation, think for a moment before speaking. Think about how you want to come across, because you don't want to turn him off before you even get started. You can always begin a conversation by asking the other person if they have time to talk. Using Step #1, you can say any of these words in a neutral tone:

- "What's going on? You seem upset. I don't want to fight with you."
- "Sal, are you angry at me? We've been friends a long time, and I want to get along with you. What's up?"
- "You're a good friend Tim. I care about you and LuAnn, and I don't want us to fight. Tell me what's going on so we can fix this."

You can change the outcome

Both people can influence the direction of most conversations. How you approach the other person and how you respond can and usually does affect the outcome. If you aren't sure how to start a conversation, you can always use Step #1 language or something similar to get it going.

If you begin with a positive approach, one that "wants to get along," you will bring that positive attitude to the discussion, and hopefully the other person will respond in kind. However, it is always possible that they may not react as you hope. If so, try not to be insulted, hurt, or defensive.

When your immediate reaction is negative or defensive, the conversation pretty much ends there. It is essentially over because in the next moment, the discussion is most likely not headed in a positive direction. Because the focus is on the relationship, don't make your reaction about you or your feelings being hurt. Be aware of yourself and your reaction, because if your spontaneous response is to get angry, impatient, frustrated, or negative, you are potentially making things worse and perhaps even continuing the cycle. In general, responding to someone you care about in an angry or aggressive manner is not nice or acceptable. Only you can control and change your own emotional reactions and behaviors.

If you tend to respond defensively, calmly ask the person a question to clarify how they are feeling. This gives you a few moments to collect your thoughts and gain more information about their point of view. Try questions, such as "What did you mean when you said I was being rude and defensive last week? What was I doing?" or "Why did you think I didn't want to go with you to the party?" or "Why did you think I was angry at you?"

This is similar to hitting the pause button, and it allows you to respond in a more constructive way. It buys you some time. You'll also gain a better understanding of what the other person was referring to, rather than having a quick negative reaction. If your response is not going to be helpful, it's better to delay your answer. You can always tell them you need some time to think about what they said or how to respond. And if you're sincere in your desire to get along, you have nothing to be defensive about.

Here's another example:

Marissa: "I want you to be more supportive."

Brian: "I am supportive. Stop telling me I'm not supportive. You always say that."

This type of back and forth can go on endlessly in some relationships. Instead of becoming defensive, Brian should ask Marissa what she means when she says she wants him to be more supportive. Instead of getting defensive or needing to be right, he could ask for clarification, if only because of his desire to improve the relationship. She can also volunteer to elaborate on what she is asking of him without being critical.

Communicating like this may be new for both of you, and those quick, knee-jerk reactions can sometimes seem ingrained in our brains. Give it time and stay patient. You may want to remind yourself beforehand to not be disappointed if the other person doesn't respond as positively as you would have liked to your efforts.

Remember, if you approach and/or respond to someone differently, you can change the outcome. Take time to collect your thoughts—even sleep on it, if necessary. Then express yourself calmly and respectfully, using the language of Step #1.

"When my partner is upset with me, I think to myself, 'Is that how I want him to feel?' It reminds me to be more compassionate and kind, instead of getting defensive."

Chapter Five

STEP # 2: "I AM GOING TO BE KIND."

Step #2 in plain English:

"I am going to be kind, not mean or sarcastic."

It would be great if all relationships used Step #2 in their daily communication. If you already do speak kindly toward each other, then this step is merely a validation of the way you communicate. If you are positive communicators, good for you!

Kindness creates a safety net that builds trust between you.

> Your kindness reassures the important people in your life that you are there for them and they can feel safe with you. This is the *only* way trust can begin to build between you and others. With trust comes better communication, hope, and ultimately conflict resolution. You must take responsibility for how you treat others, which includes being kind.

Kindness directs how you will speak to them, how you will speak about them to others, and how you will treat them going forward, all in an effort to have a better relationship. You want to be a thoughtful and respectful person.

If you are not typically kind with your words or your attitude, and instead tend to be mean-spirited, angry, impatient, or arrogant, the person on the receiving end of your unkind words or attitude may feel any of the following:

- You don't care about me.
- You don't like me or respect me.
- You don't value me.
- You don't make me feel safe.
- You don't have my back.
- You don't want to be close to me.
- I can't trust you.

If they don't feel protected and comfortable being close to you, they will feel unsafe and vulnerable. These negative feelings cause distance and conflicts in relationships. Simply being kind reinforces that the other person is important to you and that they are safe around you.

Are you nicer to strangers?

Often we do and say stupid, bad, or unkind things to the people we are closest to and care about the most. Can you think of a time when you treated a family member badly? Are you nicer to other people, those outside of your most important, close relationships?

We all tend to say hurtful things to those close to us, as if we are following one set of rules for those we care about the most and a different set of rules for everyone else. This is not uncommon, and it happens because we typically react instinctively (we "let our hair down") with those closest to us. We believe the other person should understand us, and we don't necessarily have to think before speaking when we're around them.

Unfortunately, this type of thinking fosters negative communication that can be offensive and hurtful. Going forward, pay attention not only to what you say, but also to how you say it. Then observe how those around you respond to your comments.

By implementing Step #1 ("I want to get along with you, not fight, and be closer to you") and Step #2 ("I will be kind"), you can begin to have a more positive and trusting relationships. Think about this: Why would you want to treat someone who is important to you in an unkind manner?

Yikes. Do you say things like...?

These comments are often said in close relationships, not intending to be hurtful, but to communicate something. Unfortunately, they can still sting.

- "You're wearing that? Why?"
- "You're so inconsiderate. You don't care about anyone but yourself."

- "What do you *do* all day? You don't do anything I ask you to do."
- "You're repeating yourself again."
- "Hurry up. You're always so slow."
- "Why would you say/do that? You're so stupid sometimes."

Of course, at times, all of these comments could be taken as harmless, even humorous, depending on the relationship between the speaker and the person on the receiving end. Regardless of how a comment is intended, here's a good rule: It's not nice to speak to or about someone, especially someone important to you, in a judgmental, hurtful, or unkind way. And if you say it in jest, take notice if it seems to bother them. Think about how you like others to speak to you, and then follow your own advice.

Over time, even seemingly benign negative comments can hurt a great deal and create distance between people in relationships. Being more sensitive and aware of how you speak to the important people in your life is critical.

Bottom line: If you want to have a better relationship built on trust, a constant stream of teasing or the negative comments made in passing should stop.

Example of Step #2: When Teasing Hurts:
Sticks and Stones Do Hurt Sometimes

This is a problem in many relationships. One person teases the other, thinking it's funny, or uses teasing to make a point

54

indirectly. In many situations, the person on the receiving end doesn't find the teasing funny at all. No one likes being the target of another person's nasty jokes.

"My brother and I have a close relationship. We see each other a lot because we have a lot of the same friends. He has a great sense of humor, and usually he's a pretty funny guy. He's often the center of attention at parties. He says he likes having his little sister around, but he also makes jokes about me, both when we're alone or in front of other people, and usually I don't think they're funny. He likes to tease me and calls it "innocent kidding," but I don't like the constant teasing, and I get upset. When he does this, sometimes I get annoyed and become quiet, and other times I may lash out and say something nasty back to him. I feel like I need to protect myself, so I fight back by being mean. He seems surprised when I snap back at him, but I'm not sure what else to do in that moment."

How to make Step #2 work:

The only thing that matters is that this person is hurt by her brother's teasing sense of humor. So whether he or anyone else thinks his jokes are funny is irrelevant.

Let's look at how to apply the Relationship Protocol. In Step #1, her brother likes spending time together. He cares about his sister, wants to get along, and seems not to want to hurt her feelings. Now in Step #2, if he is going to be kind, he needs to stop teasing her. Here's why: We know that his teasing upsets her, which, according to Step #2, is not being kind, and because she matters to him (Key Element #2), he needs to stop this behavior.

Whether she is overly sensitive also doesn't matter. If he intends to continue having a close relationship with his sister, he needs to

55

begin paying more attention to her feelings. For this moment, it is *only* about her hurt feelings, which he's ignoring. If, in fact, she is overly sensitive, that issue will come up later.

Here's how it changes: It is the sister's role to attempt to tell her brother in a positive way that she finds his jokes hurtful. The conversation can take place in private. It could be in person or on the phone, but not via texting, because that could be misunderstood and it's too impersonal. She needs to ask him in one or two sentences to please stop teasing because it bothers her. Hopefully, he will apologize or at least make an effort to stop the teasing. Either way, she will hopefully feel better, having thoughtfully expressed her feelings and advocated for herself. We all need to feel comfortable and safe in our close relationships, not feel that we must be on guard or need to protect our feelings from those close to us.

The sister's lashing out and being mean to her brother is her way of defending against hurt feelings. She can also apologize for lashing out at him. He may have interpreted the negative retorts as more fuel for his teasing. He may also view her as a willing participant in the "harmless" teasing cycle, as their way of joking with each other. This is an example of how negative behaviors can become a functional form of communication, but lead to negative, unconstructive results.

Some people don't understand the sensitive side of others. If someone is making fun or being negative and seemingly unaware that their behavior is hurtful, then they should be informed. After you establish a line of what doesn't feel good, you can alert others more easily, and they will begin to better understand the kinds of things that hurt your feelings. In this situation, if her brother continues teasing, she can pull him aside and ask him nicely again to knock it off, or she can just walk away and ignore it or simply choose to avoid his company. Another viable option is for her to tolerate and laugh along with the jokes. However, this works only if she truly believes they are harmless (not intended as mean putdowns) or jokes back with him.

Some people tease because they are angry, and this is their way of getting back at you or someone else. It is important to bring these things to the surface and talk about them using Steps #1 and #2. If you think teasing is their way of expressing anger at you, ask them about it. See chapter 8 for suggestions for conversation starters.

If both people are OK with joking around, then there's no problem. Yet when jokes, snipes, and teasing are consistently used as putdowns and they sting, then it's a problem. If you are not comfortable with ongoing teasing, you have a responsibility to respectfully let the other person know how you feel so they learn your limits.

On the other side of that situation, be aware that while some of your teasing comments may appear mild, benign, and even funny to the other person, you may be hurting their feelings, making them angry, and unintentionally pushing them away. So pay attention and notice their reactions.

Is there some truth to your harsh comments?

What if you are not sure how to bring up topics without being abrupt, sarcastic, or mean? It starts with "zooming out" and taking a moment to think about what you want to say and how you want to come across.

Ask yourself:

- What's their takeaway from the conversation?
- How do I want the other person to feel when I am done speaking?

Consider the tone of your voice, speak more thoughtfully, and use the Relationship Protocol as a guide. Stay away from snide, mocking, or sarcastic comments, because those kinds of remarks will never make anyone feel closer to you. Instead, they will push them further away.

But what if you think the other person is inconsiderate or lazy, or you really don't like what they are wearing and you want to tell them? Before engaging in that conversation, think about the two questions above. What is your motivation? Think carefully about your intentions. If you know the other person will be hurt by your comments, perhaps you shouldn't say anything, because it will derail the relationship you want to build. Decide whether this comment is important enough to be mentioned. If not, let it go.

If you decide that this is an important subject to be addressed, be thoughtful about how you use your words. Speak respectfully, choose words carefully, and use a softer, nonaggressive tone. If you want to have a better relationship, you are going to have to be kind and more thoughtful (Step #2). Start with language from Step #1 to set the stage for a more positive conversation coming from a caring place, and then calmly describe their behavior, words, or appearance and how it makes you feel.

Oops. It just slipped out!

What if you say something hurtful, and you realize it even as the words are coming out of your mouth? As soon as you can, tell the other person that you realized what you said (or did) may not have been kind or nice. Your role in that moment is to own it, acknowledge that you are now aware of how you spoke to them, and if need be, apologize.

This can be an important turning point. It shows that you care enough about them to stop the action and acknowledge what took place. This may be a new response on your part, which also shows them you are capable of change. They now witness firsthand that you are putting effort into being more self-aware. If they respond positively, you then experience how easily you can effect positive changes in your relationship. If they react negatively, don't get discouraged, because this new self-awareness will continue to be helpful for the relationship going forward.

Quick to anger?

Would you describe yourself or someone close to you as an angry person? Is anger your main emotion? Many people have limited emotional range. They don't necessarily express the underlying feelings of sadness, frustration, or hurt outwardly, but they definitely know how to express their anger. And when they get angry, their typical reaction is to blow up, erupt out of control, or let off some steam.

Think of it like this: Pretend that a person who expresses only anger cannot see color; they see only black and white. They live in a narrow, limited world with no variations of color. Yet as soon as they allow themselves to experience a wider range of emotions— such as hope, sadness, disappointment, fear, embarrassment, and joy—their life gradually becomes more open, and they begin to experience colors. When we open up to other emotions, we live a fuller, richer life.

When people label themselves as angry, or they define themselves in that way, anger and/or negativity are typically their familiar knee-jerk responses to many things. They may walk around with a resentful, off-putting attitude, keeping everyone at a distance and closing themselves off. For the most part, angry people wear their anger as armor to protect themselves from other feelings, such as vulnerability, sadness, or hurt.

Some individuals are quick to react, and they blame others for their own emotional reactivity. They often function in patterns of extremes and seem unpredictable. It could be that one moment they are happy, but angry and unhappy the next. If you behave in a somewhat erratic or explosive manner, please don't focus your emotional unhappiness on the other person. This may be your problem to work on, not theirs. Make an effort to determine what caused your mood change and try to find a means of understanding and controlling your emotions in a healthier way. By understanding what may have triggered the sudden change, you can begin to control your reaction.

Before or during an angry outburst, you can always use the language of Step #1. You can say, "I don't want to fight with you;

I want to get along." You can add, "I'm not sure what else to say, but I'm trying to control my temper" or "I'm really angry now, but I don't want to explode because you're important to me" or "Let me take a break and think about it and calm down." If you tell the other person you need time to collect your thoughts, be sure to reassure them that you will come back. Don't just walk away; be considerate of their feelings too.

If you get angry often, make an effort to be more aware of yourself in the moment when these angry feelings start.

- Take pause. Breathe. Count slowly to ten.
- Remove yourself from the situation if you can, and ask yourself before reacting:
  - ❑ Why am I so upset?
  - ❑ What are the feelings underneath?
- Most often something has made you frustrated or someone has hurt your feelings. It may have been building, and you haven't been dealing with whatever has been going on.
- See chapter 13 for more information on stress and self-awareness.

Let the Relationship Protocol steps be your script for communicating when you are upset. You don't have to reinvent the wheel. Rely on those words and use them during tough, intense moments. If you let it, this model can work for you.

As you continue to read more about Steps #3 and #4, you will gain a better understanding of how to address conflicts or concerns in a more constructive and respectful way. Other chapters talk about stressors, self-awareness, and stumbling blocks. Use this information to change the way you react to people and situations.

Getting angry pushes people away. You can decide right now to be a less reactive, more considerate person, especially to the important people in your life. Keep in mind that exploding with anger is unhealthy communication. It never feels good to be on the receiving end of someone's outburst. If you cannot control your explosiveness, consider seeking professional guidance. It will help you understand how and what emotional triggers set you off.

Example of Step #2: Communication between Friends
in Need of Repair: "I'm Confused. What Did I Do?"

Here is an example of someone on the receiving end of a person who often responds explosively.

"My friend is always getting into my personal business. She always wants to know whom I'm spending time with, and she gets mad at me if I hang out with anyone else. She doesn't tell me she's mad or upset, but instead she makes a scene. She either gets angry or starts yelling at me, accusing me of being a mean person, or she hangs up on me abruptly when I call and ignores me. I don't even know what I've done half the time."

This is an example of someone who doesn't know how to communicate feelings. The friend appears to come from an insecure place and may be unsure about her relationship with you. Her behavior is certainly unkind and not constructive. This is essentially the friend's problem, and your role is to help your friend become aware of how her emotional reaction affects you. If she is important to you and you want to continue the relationship, you need to sit down and have an honest conversation with her. During that conversation, you can model how you want her to speak to you when she's upset (Step #2).

Here's a good way to model positive communication:

1. Tell her you want to make time to talk. Ask her for a convenient time.

2. **Note:** Try to have a face-to-face conversation because otherwise you can miss important communication cues.

3. Begin by telling your friend that she is important to you and how much her friendship means to you (Key Element #2).

4. Let her know in a calm tone that you want to get along with her and not fight with her (Steps #1 and #2). Explain that when she gets mad, her reactions are very hurtful, and they make it difficult for you to be her friend.

5. Tell her that you don't like to be yelled at or hung up on. Nobody does.

You can explain that you like having her as a friend, but you won't tolerate her angry behavior any longer. She needs to make some changes and communicate in a nicer way when she's upset. You want her to understand that you have other friends and you want to spend time with them too. Hopefully, she can learn to be OK with your other relationships and/or try to communicate her feelings differently.

Are you out of control or abusive?

If your temper scares those around you, rethink your answer to the above question. You are attempting to build safety in your relationships using the Relationship Protocol, not fear. No one should be frightened of another person's anger or rage.

When you are upset and having a tantrum or fit, and if

- you are completely irrational and not in control of your emotions;
- you are physically or verbally abusive to another person; and/or
- they are afraid of you and the way you behave or express your emotions,

this is not acceptable. If there are times when the other person is afraid of you, your relationship is heading in the wrong direction. You must focus on changing this behavior immediately. You may need to seek professional help.

Are you not nice on purpose?

Some people don't express negative feelings directly, yet their actions or behaviors and their words most definitely elicit angry, frustrating feelings in others. For example:

- "I am so tired of my wife trying to pin me down on when I'll be home from work, so I hedge. I tell her I'll be home at seven o'clock, but I don't get home before eight-thirty. I say it just to get her off my back. She gets annoyed because she's made dinner, and it's now cold. I act like I'm innocent, as if I didn't do it on purpose, even though I actually did create the problem. Guess it's time to be honest with her about my feelings. Maybe we can work it out so I don't feel so trapped."

- "Sometimes when I'm in a bad mood, I watch myself say things to my mother that aren't very nice. I know I had a bad day, and I see that I'm upsetting her, but I don't stop myself. I don't just walk away. I set her up to get angry with me because I keep it going, or I pick a fight. I intentionally make the situation worse. I realize now I should go back to her and apologize. I have to take responsibility for my behavior because I am being hurtful and not sensitive to someone I care about. I also need to pay attention and not behave this way in the future."

In both of these examples, these individuals know, somewhere inside themselves, that their negative behavior is going to stir things up. This kind of dishonesty can become a passive-aggressive pattern of relating to others. It creates distance, causes tons of conflict, and leaves behind a path of hurt and fury. This way of behaving is also the antithesis of the RP model, which asks you to take ownership of your words and actions and to be kind.

In the first example, the husband who hedges on what time he'll be home is being intentionally disrespectful. He can choose whether or not to discuss openly how he feels with his wife. Either way, he still needs to change his reactions in the future. In the second example, this person is aware of how their behavior incites their mother. Again, this toxic behavior must stop immediately. It is rude and even cruel to treat someone in an intentionally aggressive way. A humble apology would be a great start.

Another common cause of indirect conflict is when someone repeatedly blames others for things that are actually their responsibility. For example, someone might say, "It's your fault that I drank too much last night," instead of taking responsibility and saying, "I drank too much." Or they might say, "You made me forget my wallet," rather than owning it: "I forgot my wallet." These examples may sound elementary, but when this lack of responsibility is repeated over and over again, it inevitably leads to a lack of trust and more destructive communication.

Communicate in an honest but respectful way.

When you behave in a manner that's intended to evoke negative emotions in someone you care about, you are heading down the wrong path. You are not valuing them or your relationship (Key Element #2). It's never too late to change. Use the Relationship Protocol to help you.

The message of being kind and respectful is about wanting to get along, and it comes from a place of strength, not weakness. You are promising that you will no longer use passive aggression, intimidation, manipulation, innuendo, or harsh words as weapons. If you tend to get loud, curse, resort to name calling, yell, bully, mock, bicker, or make sarcastic comments or negative gestures, you will make an effort to no longer do so intentionally. Going forward, pay attention to how you communicate and be more self-aware to better understand the things that set you off and how to deal with them in the future.

Sarcasm. Ouch!

If a relationship is healthy with good communication, sarcasm can be harmless. It's used purely in a joking way to poke fun, and it can be funny and entertaining for both people.

However, when there are conflicts in close relationships, sarcasm or sarcastic joking is never OK. Communication becomes confusing and gets misinterpreted, and issues are stirred up.

Why does this happen? Sarcasm has underlying negative messaging. It goes against the Relationship Protocol's concept of creating a safe environment, building a better relationship, and being kind.

Let's break it down: When one person is mean, snippy, or sarcastic to another person, it is typically intended to hurt the other person. And when both individuals are experts at sarcasm, nothing good or healthy comes out of it. Sarcasm in a conflicted relationship is always a distancing tool, and it represents the opposite of building trust and closeness.

People who use sarcasm as their primary way of relating to someone else usually find Step #2 a bit difficult. It seems easier to keep doing whatever they'd like, even if it hurts or bothers others. But in the end, a little effort and some kindness will always win out.

Unfortunately, some relationships are built solely on sarcasm and they are in a survival mode. By all accounts, the two individuals are typically unhappy and not doing well. They are often in a negative cycle that spirals out of control during conflicts. They are so invested in the dysfunctional communication that they can't see their way out of the turmoil. Both parties usually report being embarrassed at their own behavior, yet they are unsure how to change these habits. The individuals also fear being vulnerable if their efforts to change fail. For them, change is a risk, not a constructive step. Change will come slowly, with a few bumps in the road, but when it does, it will be well worth the effort.

The next few examples will show that, with the Relationship Protocol as your guide, change is possible if you want it badly enough. And don't wait for the other guy. You need to step up and be the change.

Example of Sarcasm in a Long-Term Relationship:
"Do We *Really* Have to Be Nice?"

Two brothers came for help at the request of their wives. These brothers primarily communicated with each other using sarcastic digs, cutting humor, and general negativity. Whether they were alone or around others, they always talked to each other by making insulting comments. They had been communicating this way since childhood, because this was how family members spoke to one another while they were growing up. It's what they described as their "unfortunate family legacy," and they wanted to change it for sake of their children.

When told about the Relationship Protocol, they liked the idea of having a guide, but they didn't like Step #2. After hearing, "I am going to be kind, not mean or sarcastic," they both, in unison, said, "No way!" and laughed hysterically. What they were really acknowledging was that they didn't know how to talk to each other without a mean dig or an unkind word. However, they also knew they were modeling poor communication for their children, and this made them both uncomfortable and motivated.

With further probing, they both admitted being hurt by the other's continual negative comments and that both were guilty of perpetuating the cycle. As brothers, they were in survival mode. Both had completely turned away from the relationship and only saw what was wrong with the other one. Still, they spoke honestly about the frustration, rage, and hurt they each experienced. Neither brother felt good about himself or how he behaved.

When asked to imagine how their family members and friends might feel after spending time with them, they became very sad. They understood that most people are uncomfortable in the company of individuals who are outwardly hostile and overtly critical toward each other. This also became a motivating factor.

They began by focusing on themselves as individuals and their own negative behavior. When they stopped waiting for the other brother to take the lead, they were nicer and talked about valuing each other and not taking the other for granted. They told each other how they wanted to be treated better and were encouraged to do so (Step #2).

As brothers, they made a promise to shift their thinking (Key Element #2) and committed to try the Protocol (Key Element #1). They were amazed at how quickly they saw positive changes, and they expressed hope and surprise at how fast things started to improve. They've had their ups and downs and, understandably, needed to work hard at changing their communication style for a few solid months before real change occurred. Over time, they have grown to trust each other and not make hurtful comments, and they relied on the Relationship Protocol whenever they needed a boost. Today they get along much better, their relationship is healthier, and their communication is sarcasm-free.

Example of Step #2: Using Kindness: Delete the Sarcasm

"I told her I'm trying. I'm trying to be better, get along better, and do the things that she wants to do when we spend time together. But I also told her that I feel like she's not meeting me halfway. I wasn't sarcastic, probably for the first time in a long while. I spoke the truth in a nice way, without an attitude or tone, and she finally realized that I was being genuine. I can't believe it, but then she apologized to me for still being nasty and untrusting. I was shocked! She admitted that she didn't trust my nonsarcastic kindness at first, but it was a great feeling when she did believe me. It took some time and a few encounters for her to see that my reactions have definitely changed."

This is the Relationship Protocol working. It is amazing how surprised people are when they see how making a small change often leads to bigger positive results. Little things, such as making a consistent effort to speak nicely or to speak without an attitude, are often all it takes to change the bad pattern. The other person will eventually notice your efforts if you stay with it, even if initially their reaction doesn't change. It might take a little time, but it feels good to be nice. If they pick up on it and begin speaking more sensitively to you, that's an even bigger bonus.

But I didn't mean it

When you realize you said or did something hurtful or unkind to the other person, even if it was unintentional, it is *your* responsibility to acknowledge it as soon as possible. If you want a better relationship, ask, "Did I just hurt your feelings?" If so, quickly and honestly apologize. This shows the other person that they matter to you and that you care about them and their feelings. By stepping up, you are helping your relationship move forward, even if it feels awkward at first. And if there is a conflict between you, then you are also demonstrating "I want to get along with you *more than I want to be right*. I want to be closer, and I am going to be kind." The conflict takes a back seat to wanting to get along and not hurt the other person. Keep paying attention and make that effort to own your words and actions. There's more about this topic in the next chapter.

Body language cues

You can also come across as mean, disconnected, or not nice through your nonverbal behavior. Nonverbal messaging can be just as frustrating, upsetting, and confusing as verbal communication and negative behavior. Just because it's silent doesn't mean it has less impact or is kind.

Nonverbal actions used to express anger or frustration include when you

- stop speaking to the person;
- ignore them;
- intentionally withdraw to punish them;
- do subtle and hurtful actions to manipulate and cause upset;
- make negative facial expressions or use negative, closed-off body language, such as rolling your eyes while they are speaking, or sit facing away from them with your arms tightly crossed; or
- shut down and turn off, seeming to be annoyed, with no verbal communication.

If any of these nonverbal behaviors occur in your relationship, try to talk about them and stop them from continuing. These nonverbal behaviors are in direct opposition to what you are trying to achieve in your relationship. Be responsible for your actions, and if you have difficulty expressing yourself, use the steps as your guide. It is critical to own your feelings and respond appropriately and kindly.

It's a simple concept: Let the other person know that they are important enough for you to become a better communicator and more self-aware. Changing your negative behavior, choosing your words more carefully, and just being kind shows them you care.

You are part of the solution

You have the power to change your relationship by changing how you communicate, behave, and react to the important people in your life.

Be thoughtful about who you want to be in your relationship. Remember, change has to start somewhere, and that somewhere is with you.

If you begin relating differently—being cheerful or kind—you instantly change the negative energy to a healthier, more positive way of communicating. You can, if you like, tell others that you're not going to be careless with your words or sarcastic anymore because you want to have a better relationship. You can ask them to follow suit after seeing your efforts to be more positive. However, if you're uncomfortable talking about your decision, take responsibility and start behaving in a more positive manner. See what happens.

Don't jab back when someone makes a sarcastic or negative comment. Break the negative communication cycle by staying focused on the relationship. Be part of the solution. Change may be subtle at first, but all positive efforts are encouraged.

And when you notice the good stuff...

When you observe the other person's efforts—no matter how small—to be nicer or more communicative, tell them. Perhaps they have spoken to you differently or behaved in a more considerate way. If you want that helpful, kind behavior to continue, don't just think it, say it. It's important to acknowledge and appreciate another person's efforts. And remember, compliments can be contagious!

Good news: Positive communication cycles build and grow just as quickly as negative ones.

The Relationship Protocol components review

These are the Key Elements:

1. A commitment to making an effort to use the Relationship Protocol, even during challenging times.

2. Shifting your "I" thinking to a relationship focus—an "us" focus—and turning toward the other person; valuing them.

The Key Elements are critical to your success using the Relationship Protocol. Keep them in the back of your mind, setting the tone for how you think about your relationship and how you keep the positive momentum going. Remind yourself that this person is important to you.

And here are the steps so far:

Step #1: I want to get along with you. I want to be closer to you, and I don't want to fight with you.

Step #2: I am going to be kind, not mean or sarcastic.

With the first two steps of the Relationship Protocol, you are making statements about the new, positive direction of the relationship.

You are now

- placing more focus on the relationship, appreciating the other person and what goes on between the two of you;

- opening up the lines of communication to make it even more positive and constructive;

- shifting your energy to a relationship focus, and your words (Step #1) demonstrate this new direction;
- developing safety in your relationship, allowing it to grow due to the positive communication between you, which is more thoughtful and respectful.

Steps #1 and #2 also enable hope and trust to come into your relationship.

When conflicts arise, as they do in all close relationships, you can use the Step #1 statements to help you defuse and de-escalate negative situations, often even before they start.

Remember, *what* you say (Step #1) and *how* you say it (Step #2) can influence and change the outcome of a conversation.

Next:

Steps #3 and #4 are more interactive. They tend to facilitate a deeper and more lasting change. These steps help to promote a stronger connection between you, building more trust, so your relationship can continue to grow and stay strong and healthy.

"We use Step #3 all the time. We stop each other and say, 'What happened? Why are you upset?' This stops everything from going any further. Now we even laugh about it sometimes! Things just don't feel as heavy as before."

Chapter Six

STEP #3: "I WILL NEVER DO ANYTHING TO INTENTIONALLY HURT YOU."

STEP # 3 in plain English

"I will never do anything to intentionally hurt you."

You can add "from now on", if you have done hurtful things in the past.

This important step helps to strengthen the trust between you and the other person, and it solidifies the foundation of your relationship. It's an action step that demonstrates two things: I am paying attention to you, and you matter to me.

Say it: "I will never do anything to intentionally hurt you."

You are saying that *your intentions from here on* are to be fully responsible for your words and your actions. You are promising to make an effort to be more self-aware and accountable, because you want the other person to begin trusting in your relationship and in you.

The key word here is *intention* to do no harm. You are not fixing anything or solving problems. However, you are continuing to build trust and focus primarily on valuing the relationship and the important person in your life. Step #3 has a few different components, but it all centers on being well intentioned.

To put Step #3 into action, you must be aware of the other person's reaction to you. Perhaps during a conversation you notice that the other person is getting upset, or you pick up some behavioral cues; maybe the other person acts sad, angry, or hurt, or they roll their eyes or stand up and abruptly walk away from you. These cues indicate that the other person is clearly unhappy.

Now let's apply the steps when something like the aforementioned happens.

Because you are now focused on getting along (Step #1), being kind (Step #2), and valuing the other person (Key Element #2), your role when you notice the other person's negative reaction is to immediately stop the action. In that moment or soon after, you stop whatever you were saying or doing and immediately ask a question about what you just observed.

You might ask the following: "What just happened?" or "You seem sad, angry, irritated. What's happening?" or "Did I say or do something that upset you?" or "What's going on?" Ask them a question that gets to the heart of about what you observed, and keep it as short as these suggestions.

You stop immediately because what *you* were saying or doing in that moment now becomes irrelevant and unimportant. What matters now is only that the other person (whom you want to get along with, be kind to, and not intentionally hurt) is now unhappy or upset. Your focus automatically changes. It moves immediately from what you were saying and shifts your focus to them and their reaction because you want to improve your relationship and you certainly don't want them to be upset.

Here are just some specific changes to watch for:

- **Facial and verbal expression:** Avoiding eye contact and looking away, scowling, making a sad face, tearing up, rolling eyes, or changing tone of voice, which may get stronger, more forceful, louder, or perhaps much softer.
- **Emotions:** Angry, hurt, sad, tearful, closed off, confused, shocked/surprised in a negative way, sighing, or moaning.
- **Behavior:** Abruptly leaves, ignores you, starts crying, crosses arms, physically turns away, posture sinks in, stands with hand on hip while looking annoyed, hangs up the phone abruptly, or starts rapidly tapping foot as if agitated.

- **Energy between you:** Shifts from calm and/or OK to feeling tense, awkward, uncomfortable, strained, pressured, or nervous.

Don't assume you know what the person's behavior means, and don't ignore their behavior. Simply ask, "What's happening? You seem upset, angry, ...?" Hit the pause button and check in.

Here are more good reasons to pay attention and stop the action:

The by-product of acknowledging their feelings in that moment (or soon after) is that you validate the other person. It shows them that you are paying attention and that they are more important than whatever you were saying or doing at that time. This is reassuring to the person on the receiving end of that interaction.

Embrace the power of Step #3

Step #3 gives hope and defuses conflict. There are two reasons why this is true:

1. This step directly impacts the future of your relationship.

Each time you stop the action and apologize, you are acknowledging the other person's feelings, respecting them, and valuing them. This small, caring gesture goes a long way because it instantly injects some hope into your relationship, focuses on the importance of the relationship, and sets the tone for trust to grow.

In time, once you begin to trust each other and communicate better, you can begin to talk about the problems and concerns in your relationship. When you have a stronger, more comfortable relationship, it becomes easier and safer to communicate about issues that were once off-limits. The Relationship Protocol communication tools are then used to guide you through the interactions.

Using Step #3 at any point in your relationship will always remind the other person that they are important to you. The model is a framework that goes from teaching you how to talk to each other and defuse conflict to becoming a guide for communication and discussing your problems. This comment explains the point further: "I appreciate when you apologize instead of getting angry. It really helps me because it shows me that you care, and that's the most important thing to me."

2. This is how you defuse and stop the escalation!

By being more self-aware and paying attention to the other person, you now have an opportunity to defuse, de-escalate, and remain calm during all potentially tough interactions. Most downward spirals can go from zero to one hundred in lightning speed. But if you notice things that are happening between you and address them immediately, you have a good chance of stopping the momentum of the escalation. If you're both working on paying attention, you have an even greater shot at defusing the disagreement before it starts. It takes two to continue an escalating argument, so value the other person more than investing in the negativity or needing to stay on your point.

When you begin to understand and believe that your relationship is all about getting along, you will clearly see that it's never about being right. This is where the expression "relationship before content" comes into play. Getting along, building trust, and supporting each other's feelings are much more important than being right, fixing problems, or finishing your point. If you buy into this Relationship Protocol belief system, you will be more apt to stop escalations before they even begin.

You may have a difficult time letting go of being right or wanting to continue what you were saying when it is infinitely more important to stop, check in, and perhaps apologize. This is where most people get stuck. So think about this: Why is that so important to you? Is this a competition, a need to be recognized, or perhaps some stubbornness getting in your way? Does winning the point or being right really matter as much if you want to have a better relationship? Put this need to be right, to finish your point, or to focus on yourself or your needs aside, and see how you can build a better "together."

This step is humbling and requires some self-control and self-awareness. There's more about self-awareness in chapter 13.

You need to observe both yourself and the other person during your interactions in order to be successful with Step #3.

Why do you stop right now?

What is the value of stopping whatever you were saying or doing?

> The relationship between you is more important and it comes before anything else in that moment. This is how trust begins to build and how conflicts get defused before they have a chance to escalate.

Important note: In healthy relationships, it's important to pay attention and express interest in the other person's feelings. Your energy and focus is on them (Turning toward them as in Key Element #2). By sincerely acknowledging their feelings, you are showing them that they matter. Don't make it about you; let it be about the other person in that moment.

You want a better relationship, so you stop and ask calmly with sincerity and kindness, "What happened?" Ask them,

- "What's going on?"
- "What did I miss? You seem upset."
- "What's up, Francine? I really want to know."
- "Did I do something that upset you? If I did, I'm sorry."

If you're lucky, the other person will then tell you, "You did XXX, and that bothered me" or "You used that condescending tone with me" or "I'm ticked that you mentioned XXX when I told you I didn't want to talk about it!" This may take practice and repeated attempts, but you can't give up. Listen while they explain what was happening in that moment for them.

They may say, "I'm unhappy, but it has nothing to do with you." (That's always nice to hear!) And it truly may not have anything to do with you, and/or you may be misreading the situation. So stop the action, check in, and see what's going on.

In a word: Apologize

If after you check in, the other person tells you that you did something to upset them, *your next and only response to them is to immediately* **apologize.**

- Do not continue what you were saying, making your point, or focusing on being right.
- Do not explain why you did or said something, because that information is not important at that moment.
- Just *stop!*
- It is only about them and their feelings now. Your focus is on them.
- Don't analyze or overtalk.
- *Just apologize for hurting their feelings, upsetting them, or doing whatever caused the problem in the first place.*

Your willingness to show them you care will go a long way, much more than you realize now.

The simplest way to look at this step is to ask yourself, "Do I want them to be upset or unhappy?" Your answer should be that you do not want them to be upset or hurt.

If you don't want the other person to feel badly, even if it was unintentional, or you don't fully understand their hurt feelings, you still apologize. Why? *Because more than anything else, you don't want them to feel that way.* This is an important part of the motivation behind Step #3.

Example of How a Quick Apology Goes a Long Way

Rachel (clearly in jest): "Aren't I the best baker? I love baking cookies."

Jesse (responding in jest): "Well, you would be if you brought me the cookies with some milk."

Rachel (sounding annoyed and hurt): "Are you kidding? You are so ungrateful!"

Jesse (now annoyed at her reaction): "What is your problem? Are you kidding me? Here we go. Forget it. I don't want any cookies."

If Jesse can stop himself from the knee-jerk, annoyed "Are you kidding me?" response, he may realize that a simple "I'm sorry. I was genuinely kidding" might be all that's needed to stop the conflict that is on the brink of escalating. If you don't recognize when you hurt someone's feelings or your part in the conflict, but instead get annoyed at them for being upset with you, you perpetuate a negative cycle. If you want to get along with the other person and show that you care about them, you don't want them to think you were intentionally being hurtful when, in fact, you were joking. Even if the other person is being overly sensitive, that doesn't matter at that moment. It's more important that you are responsible for your words and actions.

Pay attention

When you stop whatever you're saying and ask the other person about your observation, in that moment you also need to pay attention to yourself, your reactions, and your own feelings. If and when they tell you what's bothering them, you may disagree or have a strong negative reaction to whatever they say.

This is the most difficult and humbling part of this process.

If you want someone to trust your intentions, you need to catch yourself and be present during all interactions, focusing on getting along and being kind. So when someone tells you something that you don't like or don't want to hear, you have to change your pattern of responding. You need to be self-aware, observe yourself, and listen to them without reacting negatively or defensively.

If you react quickly or show annoyance at their reasons for being upset, you are continuing the negative cycle and not turning toward them.

Realistically, their comments may not be what you want to hear or what you expect; in fact, they may make you upset or angry. For this new phase of your relationship, make an effort to listen to the other person and take a moment to think before you automatically respond. Doing so shows your desire to get along and be closer.

These are powerful and important suggestions that can change the direction of a relationship. You have the power to make significant changes in your relationship individually and together if you take a moment to think before responding and follow the Relationship Protocol.

This is not about simply agreeing with the other person's feelings or opinions. It's about making an effort to understand and show that they matter to you.

You don't want to reject them, deny their feelings, or criticize them, because their feelings are real to them. This is an opportunity to build trust and compassion, so be aware and observe your reactions, and try not to defend yourself.

If you react negatively instead of apologizing or acknowledging the other person's feelings, just go back and apologize for your reaction as soon as you realize what you did. Apologize for your behavior that made them upset, because this was not your intention. This will begin the process of breaking the negative cycle. It's not about responding perfectly each time as much as it is about making an effort, sticking with your commitment, and taking responsibility for your part.

Show you care: Apologize

Remember the Key Elements: I am committed to making an effort (#1), and I am focused on having a better relationship and valuing you because you are important to me (#2). (You are not solving problems now, just learning how to communicate.) And the steps:

Step #1: I want to get along with you. I want to be closer, and I don't want to fight with you.

Step #2: I am going to be kind, not mean or sarcastic.

Now let's look again at Step #3: "I will never do anything to intentionally hurt you." You are essentially saying, "I want us to get along better, and I don't want to make you upset."

This is a critical differential:

- **You *are not* apologizing** for having a difference of opinion, for bringing up an important topic that they didn't want to talk about, for not wanting to watch the same TV program, movie, etc.

- **You *are* apologizing** because whatever happened between you, something that you did or said, or the way you spoke to them resulted in them getting upset. You feel badly that they are unhappy, and you apologize because they matter to you.

Apologizing doesn't change your opinion or your desire to bring up that important topic another time, and it doesn't make you feel less frustrated that the problem may still exist. This step shows the other person that you care about their feelings. The rest will come. For now, apologize and move on.

Remember, *you didn't mean to intentionally hurt them,* so your role in that moment, or as soon as you realize that you did hurt them, *is to show them that you care by apologizing.*

You must acknowledge your part if something you did caused their upset, *even if it was unintentional.* You are putting the relationship first, because they matter to you. Can you do that? This is at the heart of Step #3.

This is the time when big changes can begin to happen.

By immediately stopping the conversation, even midtopic or midsentence, and apologizing, you own your role and acknowledge their hurt out loud. You apologize and let them know, "This was not my intention." Regardless of the point you were making, when you stop and put aside that point and immediately ask them, "What happened?" you are showing that *they are your priority*. You are changing the way you speak to each other, and in that moment, you are beginning to build trust.

Not happy with their "I'm fine!" response?

It's possible that even from the beginning of the interaction, when you proudly remember to stop the action and ask the other person, "What's going on?" or "What just happened?" your moment may be dashed because you may have misread them and things are OK. They may also have a negative, knee-jerk response, saying, "Nothing happened! I'm fine." Their response is a message that you should back off. If this happens, you need to respond in a neutral, nonaggressive tone. You can say these phrases: "OK, got it" or "Guess I misread the signs, but OK" or "OK, but if something is bothering you, I hope you'll tell me." Then calmly leave it alone for now.

It's about them, not you

What if they answer your question "What happened?" by telling you that something you said or did bothered them? Or what if they approach you later and unexpectedly tell you out of the blue that they are unhappy about something you said or did earlier?

Take a moment to think about how you want to respond to either of the above scenarios and remember Step #3.

The same rules apply whether you observe something and approach the other person asking them, "What happened?" or whether the other person comes to you to discuss something that you did or said that bothered them.

In either scenario, it's best to start with an apology, whether you realized they were upset or not. You didn't do anything to deliberately hurt them, yet they are unhappy; so don't make your response about you. This particular interaction is only about their feelings of anger, hurt, or unhappiness. You may see things differently than they do, but right now, make the conversation about their feelings and let them know they matter to you. This builds the trust you want.

Suggestion: If they share a feeling with you, you can restate the feeling in your response, such as saying, "I'm sorry I made you angry" or "I didn't know you were upset last night." Using the feeling they expressed in your response demonstrates that you were listening to them.

If you don't know why they are unhappy, ask them, "What happened?" in a genuine way, and then demonstrate a sincere interest in what they are saying and how they are feeling.

Even if you are completely unaware that their feelings were hurt and it was totally unintentional, you still apologize.

For now, it's about them.

> Your thinking and response immediately shift to the other person who now appears to be unhappy or tells you that they are unhappy. It then becomes about their experience in that moment.
>
> Letting go of the point you were making, stopping yourself from proving their reaction was wrong, and not getting defensive can be undeniably difficult. Yet if you don't own your part, and take responsibility, you will get stuck in the same negative communication cycle over and over again.
>
> Your ultimate objective is about making the relationship better and breaking old patterns. Try to focus on what is happening with the other person as much as, if not more than, you pay attention to yourself and your feelings.

Apology *not* accepted?

You did what you are supposed to do. You said something potentially hurtful, and you immediately apologized. But what if the other person doesn't respond as you'd hoped. What if they aren't interested in your apology? This may happen for a number of reasons. They may not trust you or your apology, or they may still feel angry or resentful and can't get past their own feelings. It's also possible that they just don't know how to respond.

If their reply to your apology is negative, over the top, or less than the positive response you expected, make a big effort to stay on point. Do your best to not react to their negative response. Let them know you are sincerely trying to be more aware. You can express your disappointment, but don't be impatient with them, overdramatize your point, or hang onto their reaction.

Suggestion: You can ask them to help you understand why they are not accepting your apology, but be prepared to respect their answer, and don't push the point.

If you acknowledge to them that trust takes time and you're in the relationship for the long haul, they will hopefully find some comfort in your willingness to stick with the relationship even through the rough spots (Key Element #1). This also keeps the momentum moving in a positive direction instead of having a setback because they didn't respond well to your apology.

For now, remain focused on your path toward improving your relationship. In time, if you continue to make an effort and "own your stuff," the other person will begin to see that your effort is genuine. When that time comes, it will be easier and more natural for them to accept your apology. Give it time; relationship patterns don't change overnight. The journey will most likely have its ups and downs, so put on your seat belt and hang in there.

Who me? I'm never defensive

Most people have a natural tendency to attack back or get defensive when someone sounds critical, says they've done something wrong, doesn't accept an apology, or has made them angry or upset. However, because you are now more focused and interested in getting along and improving your relationship more than anything else, your next move is to be aware and pay attention to your own reactions in that moment. If reacting defensively is your typical response, this may take some time.

This bears repeating: if you feel yourself becoming annoyed, self-protective, or defensive after the other person tells you what upset them, try to stop the action (hit the pause button) and calmly ask them a question.

Ask a question that is relevant to their observation, which will accomplish two things:

1. It will give you more information and tell you why they are upset.
2. It will help you buy some time to collect your thoughts.

Some additional questions could be

- "Rebecca, why did you think I was angry last night?"
- "Please tell me why you think I acted that way on purpose?"
- "Help me understand how I hurt your feelings Tamar? I still don't understand."
- "What am I doing that makes you think I'm being defensive?"
- "I want to respond better, but it's hard when you're angry. Why are you still so mad?"

Instead, try this response

Use some neutral "I" statements in response, and don't forget Step #2 (I will be kind) and Step #3 (I will never do anything to intentionally hurt you):

- "I'm really sorry I hurt you, Maya."
- "I appreciate you telling me how you feel."
- "I see what you mean, Adam. Let me try this again..."
- "I guess maybe I was insensitive, and I'm sorry."
- "I understand your point. Even though I might not agree with it, I do respect your opinion."
- "I don't want you to feel that way. It is/was never my intention to hurt you Marley, and I apologize for what I did/said."

Step #3 can be a tough transition for many reasons. Apologizing may be difficult because it doesn't come naturally and isn't always comfortable. It's easier to evade the issue and cast blame instead. Responding defensively may be more common and comfortable for you. You may not agree with the other person's perspective, or you simply want to make your point. Maybe you rely on sarcasm as a defense mechanism to protect yourself, or you don't want to pay attention and change how you communicate; you just want to be yourself. Whether or not you fully understand the direction of the Relationship Protocol at this point, trust the process and stay with it. *This step is the most difficult, but it also has the most impact.*

When applying the Relationship Protocol method, apologizing is a critical component for developing trust and taking ownership for your behavior and actions. You must make an effort to acknowledge when you've hurt the other person as well as offer an apology when you've done or said something hurtful. Again, it's about the other person in that moment, not you. If, instead, you find yourself continuing to react defensively and would like to try to change this ingrained response, think about how the other person makes you feel in that moment. Zoom out and be curious as to why it's difficult for you to hear something that may be critical. It could be the way they speak to you, their tone, your own history, or something else that's happening. Respectfully and thoughtfully share your observations with them, and see if together you can work on this.

Example of How Not to Be Defensive: "Did I Miss Something?"

Your friend tells you he's upset with you because he felt you ignored him at the party last night. You are surprised and perhaps even annoyed at his comments because you thought you both had a good time. A common defensive answer might be "I didn't ignore you" and/or "You're just too sensitive."

When using the Relationship Protocol, some options for answering someone without defensiveness could instead be

- "Rick, I didn't know that I hurt your feelings last night. I'm sorry."
- "I didn't think I ignored you last night, but if you think I did, then I'm sorry and it wasn't intentional."
- "I certainly didn't ignore you on purpose. It wasn't intentional Tyler. I'm very sorry you felt that way."

You are apologizing because your friend *felt* you *did* ignore him, even though that was never your intention and you didn't realize he felt that way until he mentioned it. Whether or not you believe that you ignored him at the party is irrelevant. You didn't set out to intentionally hurt his feelings, and therefore you apologize (Step #3). Because you care about him and his feelings, you are letting him know he matters to you. This is how you begin to build trust. If you think your friend is being too sensitive or he misunderstood something that took place at the party, feel free to try to explain it later. Remember, only explain yourself when the person is ready to move past the hurt feelings. If not, let it go for now. Lastly, when you acknowledge a person's hurt feelings, do so with an apology and in a respectful and thoughtful way.

Stay focused and be nonreactive.

Do not react harshly or negatively to the other person's unpleasant response, whether it occurs before or after you ask, "What happened?" This is why many conflicts escalate. Both people become reactive to each other's negative reactions, comments, or perceived negative comments, and then the negative cycle gets revved up. If you're making an effort at saying or doing something positive, stay with it, even if the other person isn't quite on board yet.

Important note: If you have a strong reaction to another person's comments, take responsibility for it and apologize as soon as you become aware of your own negative response. Even if they are not ready to hear it or they think an apology is not necessary, you are responsible for your words and actions. You therefore apologize, or at least acknowledge what you did in some way. Focus on changing the energy between you, and stay on track by continuing to be self-aware and kind, following all the helpful components of the RP.

Why not just ignore it, forget it, or get over it?

Is there a downside to ignoring something you observe or avoiding the potential conflict and choosing not to ask, "What's going on?" or "What's happening?"

If the other person appears to be upset about something and you don't ask about it, in time their feelings can build up and affect the relationship. However, if their negative feelings subside, maybe they were fleeting and unimportant.

A good rule is not to jump on every observation, comment, or feeling, especially if it seems small. If you observe something that appears to be a problem for them or they bring up something negative a second time, then there may be an issue. If significant negative feelings are kept inside and not shared, the same issues will repeat, and those stuffed-down feelings may build up, simmer, pile on, and become intense.

Think of a pot full of water on the stove with the lid on. You turn on the heat, and as the water heats up, the water pressure begins to get more intense until the lid pops off the top and the water boils over. What a mess that can make! It's no different with your emotions when there is no outlet for them.

Over time, these intensely negative feelings will spill out or explode, and you may observe a change in demeanor. The other person may become resentful, ignore you, respond more negatively, or behave more impatiently, silently, angrily, sarcastically, or unhappily. A little thing may cause a blowup that appears to be out of proportion because of the pushed-down, unexpressed feelings. Negative energy that gets stuffed down can make us physically ill because it is destructive, toxic energy. Don't let that bad energy between you and the other person go unnoticed and unaddressed. Take a moment and talk about it if it seems important.

Also, pay attention and observe your own reactions and feelings. Do you tend to ignore negative feelings, stuff them down, and then explode? Do you let resentments build up? If so, make an effort to become a better communicator using the tools of the RP.

Step #3: Example of the Quiet Ones: The Bucket

Carmen reported that she and her husband, both highly educated professionals, didn't know how to communicate with each other. She said that every time they had a disagreement or something upset her, her overwhelmingly angry feelings went into a bucket. It was an imaginary bucket, but all the negatives about her husband and their relationship went into that bucket. Carmen's husband just brushed everything under the rug because he was unaware of the imaginary bucket that was filling up.

For months at a time, or even longer, the bucket would get heavier and heavier because she had no way to talk it out. She pictured herself like a hobo walking around with a bucket on a stick. When the bucket got too heavy and she couldn't carry it anymore, she'd blow, and from that moment on, everything he did was wrong. It was as if he were blamed for breathing. They fought over everything, including the kids, the dishes, money, and personal hygiene.

The couple finally decided they wanted to work on their relationship and learn to talk civilly to each other. Carmen certainly didn't like herself and how she felt when her bucket was full. She considered herself to be a good person who looked at life optimistically. Yet, when she was angry with her husband, she became someone she wasn't proud of, because she was impatient and hurtful. Her husband realized that he, too, needed to be a better communicator and more aware of what was happening between them.

Carmen learned to communicate her feelings, apologized sincerely for her past negative behavior, and used the steps to prevent her bucket from filling up. Her husband also made an effort to be more considerate and observant in their relationship.

The imaginary bucket is a good visual image of pushing your feelings down until the bucket gets too heavy and you explode. In healthy, caring relationships, both of you have responsibilities. Carmen had the responsibility to own her feelings, pay attention to the bucket filling up, and communicate her feelings thoughtfully to her husband. Her husband's responsibility required him to notice that his wife seemed unhappy and then to reach out and ask her about his observation—because he cares.

If you have a relationship with someone who tends to hold things inside, you can try to help them express themselves by using the RP tools to reduce their fears or defensiveness. You now have some skills to rely on for speaking with them in a civilized way instead of being out of control and likely to explode. Your goal is to create a better relationship where both of you are safe to express yourselves.

If your bucket tends to get heavy, decide which things are important to discuss and which should be discarded. Then use the Relationship Protocol to help you address those important issues. Refer to chapter 8 for suggestions.

Not comfortable communicating?

What if communication doesn't come easily or naturally? Maybe you've never been comfortable communicating, or you avoid potential conflicts at all cost. Do you view certain topics as risky, fearing the conversation could go on forever and it might not end well? Perhaps you weren't brought up in a family that was big on communication, or you just don't see yourself as a strong communicator. Sometimes it just seems easier to not talk about something, rather than deal with the consequences.

First of all, you're not alone. All of the above issues and concerns are very common. Many people would rather not talk about their feelings. They would rather walk on fire than upset the other person or have a possible confrontation or conflict. But look at it this way: if you choose not to address something that you observe in the other person, then you are allowing negative feelings to build up inside of them. When those feelings are finally exposed, the situation may be more emotional and thus more difficult to defuse at that point.

Yet, if you check in with them, you are more apt to be self-aware and in control of your response in that moment, versus potentially getting caught off guard. In the end, they may tell you everything is fine and your concern was all for naught. On the other side, if you are not willing to check in with yourself (more in chapter 13) and bring up something that you are feeling or thinking, no one around you will ever know what's going on. They should not have to be a mind reader to be in a relationship with you. If the issue is important, figure out a way to be more communicative (hint: use the model). This comment sums up the point: "If there's something that's bothering me and I don't bring it up, I'm hurting myself and the relationship."

In relationships where one person is significantly quieter, it often becomes the more verbal person's responsibility to be observant and lead the way for using the Relationship Protocol. Sometimes a quiet person may isolate or avoid communicating for many reasons. Talk to them about what holds them back. Reassure them that you want to get along (Step #1). You want to be their soft landing, so support their efforts to become a better communicator using the RP. In time, when they start feeling more comfortable and safe in the relationship, you will both experience closer and more satisfying communication.

If you are in a relationship where neither of you are comfortable communicating, the hope is that one of you will decide to step out of your comfort zone and begin applying the RP. If you both hold back, your relationship will not progress. It takes only one of you to make the first move, and nothing will change if you don't try. Take it one step at a time, and let the change start with you.

Conversations starters

Begin by recognizing that unless you share something that is important to you, the other person may never know your thoughts or feelings, because they cannot read your mind. Think of the Key Elements: you are committed to improving your relationship (#1), so you may need to extend yourself into new and uncomfortable territory for the sake of the relationship and for this person whom you value (#2).

- Initially, what matters most is that you're making an effort to connect, so if need be, call, e-mail, or text them. Let them know you are reaching out because they are important to you.

- Fill them in and start small: Have a brief conversation when you're not upset, and talk about your discomfort dealing with a conflict or your insecurity about expressing yourself. Talk about how this is difficult for you.

- Use the language of the steps. Ask them if it's a good time to talk. You might say, "I want to get along better (Step #1) and be a better communicator, but this is tough for me." Let them know you want to be more open, but you may need some help from them.

- Express your willingness and interest to communicate. If they talk a lot or cut you off when you are speaking, let them know with kindness. Say instead, "This is hard for me" or "This is something I might not typically talk about, so please try to let me finish what I have to say" or "I want to talk to you about something, and I need you to just listen." Your intent here is to have them hit that pause button before they respond to you.

- Be patient with them because this is a new way of communicating for both of you. They're accustomed to being the talker in the relationship, and listening may not come as naturally for them.

- Be aware of your response too, especially if they don't respond the way you wished for.

- Most important, don't give up. Keep making that effort because your relationship is worth it.

- Use the steps as a guide to give you the words and the confidence you need. Hopefully it will get easier. Check out chapter 8 for more helpful suggestions.

Thank you for sharing

If you are on the receiving end of someone who is making an effort to be more communicative or kind, be grateful. Acknowledge and encourage it. This could be a critical point, especially if this person tends to shy away from communicating. It most likely was an effort for them, and you should welcome and appreciate any effort they put forth.

A good response from you is "Thanks" or "Thanks for telling me, James." or "Thanks for making the effort," even if you don't like what the person said. If they share an emotion with you, such as "I got angry when you did XXX," simply respond by using that same emotion in your sentence: "I'm sorry you got angry when I did XXX." This lets them know you were actively listening.

Appreciate that they stepped out of their comfort zone and took a chance on expressing their emotions. If you want them to continue making that effort, respond well, or you may lose your shot. And be sincere, because if you acknowledge and reward them by supporting them, you're making things better for both of you for today and the future. Remember, you don't need to explain your point and drive it home when they share. Instead, show your appreciation for their efforts, and be a good listener. Give them their time, as much as they need.

If you realize afterward that you may have glossed over their newfound effort or that you didn't listen as well as you could have, just go back and tell them you appreciate what they did or said. Be encouraging to them, and own your slipup in that situation. Remember, it's never too late to correct a misunderstanding or to offer a positive observation.

How do you want the other person to *feel* in the relationship?

When the other person tells you something that's bothering them, take a moment before responding and ask yourself, "*Is this how I want them to feel?*" For instance, they may say you are being mean or you've hurt their feelings or you've made them feel unappreciated, worthless, or invisible. Instead of a typical quick response, which might include getting angry, proving them wrong, fighting back, shutting down, or getting defensive, why not say, "I am really sorry you thought I was mean," or whatever the complaint was.

Think of the Relationship Protocol and say, "If I want to get along with you and be kind, the last thing I want to do is make you feel something negative. Even if I'm not sure how I made you feel that way, I still don't want you to experience those bad feelings. That is never my intention, and therefore, I am very sorry I made you feel XXX."

Bottom line: Try to shift to more of a relationship focus. Connect with them in that moment when they say they are feeling badly because of something you said or did. Immediately own it, take responsibility, and apologize. If you respond compassionately, you are demonstrating caring, building trust, and defusing a potential fight. This is a critical component in quickly stopping a conflict. And to avoid this same issue in the future, ask yourself, "What do I need to do differently so the other person doesn't feel this way anymore?"

Let the content go and concentrate on demonstrating that they are important to you.

In truth, this step is not only humbling, but it can also be difficult. It requires being observant of yourself and the other person. You need to pause for self-reflection and thoughtfulness. You are not relinquishing control, giving in, folding, or being weak; you are strengthening your relationship. Step #3 is definitely not about weakness. When you both use Step #3 and apologize to each other, you are coming from a place of strength.

But what if the other person is controlling, supersensitive, overreactive

When dealing with someone who can be controlling, overreactive, untrusting, or difficult, it is even more important to stay with the model and be consistent. If you use the steps and continue to openly acknowledge and apologize each time you hurt the other person's feelings, eventually it will be obvious to both of you that you are sincerely making an effort to work on the relationship.

Here's how it works: If you continue in earnest to use the model to improve your relationship, in a few weeks or months the other person may begin to trust you and your intentions. At that point, a shift often occurs as it becomes obvious to both of you that your efforts and your intentions are pure. The other person may then begin trusting you and your intentions because you've been consistent over time. Yet what if their reactions are still the same? This is when it becomes clear that the issue may be the other person's individual problem to work on and not necessarily your problem or a relationship problem.

If they don't acknowledge the positive changes you have made, you can gently point out that you have been making a big effort, yet they still don't trust you. The hope is that once the other person experiences more trust in you, they may begin to look within to be more self-reflective. The Relationship Protocol brings issues like these to the surface—but only if you use the model consistently.

Step #3: Example of Intent:
"Can You Just Spend Some Time with Me?"

Mother to college-age daughter: "Doreen, when you're home on break from school, why don't you spend any time here? It's unacceptable and hurtful to Dad and me. You come home, and you just disappear, as if you don't want to see us at all. I'm not denying you the time with your friends, but give me a break. Can't you give us even a little bit of your time? Have dinner with us, or come out of your room. You're either with your friends or in your room talking to them."

Doreen: "Mom, this is normal. I'm just happy to see my friends, and I want to spend time with them." She starts to leave the room, obviously annoyed.

Mother: "You get so mad so fast. I bet you don't get as angry with your friends!"

Doreen: "I'm not mad, but it is annoying. I just want to see my friends. Please don't tell me that it's unacceptable. I'm really sorry if that makes you feel badly. I'm not trying to hurt anyone's feelings. I think because I'm your oldest, you just don't know that kids my age like to go out a lot and be with their friends. It's not to run away from you, I promise!"

Mother: "I didn't say you were doing it on purpose, Doreen, and maybe I shouldn't have said 'unacceptable.' I am sorry, but I want you to know that we want you to stay home with us sometimes."

Doreen: "OK, I got it. I'll spend time with you guys tomorrow night before I go out. OK?"

Mother: "Yes, thanks. That would be great!"

In this situation, the mother spoke directly to her daughter about her feelings. She described Doreen's behavior as "hurtful and unacceptable," which could have backfired, made her daughter angry, and escalated into a big argument. Using strong, definitive words can come off as controlling and off-putting to the other person. However, in this case, her daughter started to get annoyed but then stopped herself and apologized because she realized that her mother's reaction was more about feeling hurt and sad rather than being controlling. By apologizing, Doreen acknowledged that even though it wasn't intentional, going out with her friends made her mom feel badly. She also made it easier for her mom to listen to her point of view.

The mother then recognized what had occurred and subsequently apologized for her poor choice of words (*unacceptable*). In the end, the daughter was willing to compromise and set aside a little time for her parents, which made her parents happy. Doreen's decision not to get angry or defensive and then to apologize for her unintentionally upsetting behavior allowed them to resolve a potentially volatile situation, move forward, and build trust together.

But wait. We never discussed the issue!

By now you're probably wondering, what about the content, the issue that got you into this disagreement? How do you shelve the topic, your problems, and your history after you apologize or acknowledge the other person's feelings?

When you begin using the Relationship Protocol, yes, the content (and the issue, topic, problems, and your history) is initially discarded, even if there's a new conflict. The Protocol is teaching you how to talk to each other and build trust, so just for now, the focus is only on the relationship and what is happening communication-wise between you and the other person. It's not about the specific issues. It's important to acknowledge, not ignore, the topics or communication patterns that get in the way and cause conflicts. You will eventually talk about them, just not now.

Once trust grows, the rest will follow. If the topic was not important and you can both agree to let it go, then put it aside and move on. If you feel ready to tackle a small issue, give it a shot. However, if the conversation starts to "go negative," stop immediately and agree to table it until your communication skills and relationship are on a better track with the RP. It's important to wait until you are both more comfortable communicating with one another. Then you will also have a better chance at successfully discussing problems. If there has been a misunderstanding or conflict, the receiver of the apology must be able to move past their hurt and accept the apology before anything of substance is discussed.

If you want to talk about a current issue, wait until you are both calm, and use the Relationship Protocol Key Elements and Four Steps as your guide. If possible, also wait until you have some practice and positive experiences using the RP before attempting to use it with more serious problems. Chapter 11 discusses the phases of the RP and when you might be ready to tackle problems.

Before speaking, take a moment to think ahead of time about what you want to get across and how you want the other person to feel. Then speak to them in a considerate, thoughtful, and respectful manner. Remember that sometimes conflicts arise simply because we want the other person to agree with us. Be open to understanding that you may disagree; that has to be OK. If both of you are cognizant of making an effort for the sake of the relationship and of being thoughtful and kind, you may very well get through the content unscathed. If, however, things start to move in a negative direction, it's important to stop the discussion respectfully and go back to using the steps before anything escalates.

Important note: Caution is advised when discussing sensitive topics.

Be cautious and respectful if you are revisiting a sensitive topic, because it will most likely still be difficult to discuss. Stay in the present, go slowly, and start with benign, safe topics for discussion for a few weeks (or preferably months) until you have built some trust between you and have more experience using the RP. Then move on to those personal, sensitive topics when you feel confident in the relationship and there's a history of positive efforts to fall back on, should these more difficult discussions go badly.

Approach each conversation gently, and be a good observer of yourself and the other person. Notice if things seem to be going well or if they are moving off course. Check in and talk about how the discussion is going so you can defuse any potential conflicts along the way.

It's OK to shelve the issue—for now

You may not feel you have the ability to have a civilized or effective conversation about a difficult topic at this point. You may believe that it will escalate or become negative, as it has in the past. For now, it is 100 percent acceptable to delay any conversations that are of concern. This model moves along in phases as change occurs in a relationship. You will learn more about using the model and the three phases of the Relationship Protocol later. Until you have some significant practice with the model and are comfortable in the last phase of integrating the RP, it's a good idea to shelve those tougher subjects temporarily.

Communicate your concerns and decide together to put the issue aside for now. Make a list of issues and concerns to get back to at a later date. It can be helpful knowing that the issues are not being ignored, just delayed for the sake of working on your relationship.

Deciding to put off a conversation speaks to your strengths because it shows that you value your relationship and want to protect it. This is not a sign of weakness; it is an accurate commentary on the state of your relationship at that time. When your relationship is stronger, give the conversation a try, keeping the Key Elements and the steps in mind. However, if after a few attempts, you continue to be uncomfortable having the discussion, consider seeking professional help to guide you.

When things go badly, how do you recover?

If a conversation doesn't go well, ends in a fight, or begins escalating, or if one of you gets upset, try not to get too discouraged. It takes time to change the way you communicate, especially if the negative patterns have been around for a long time. It can also be difficult to remember to hit the pause button, apologize, and not react negatively when the other person tells you that you hurt them. Sometimes your discussions may not go as you planned or as you hoped they would.

Regardless of how bad it may get between you and the other person, you can *always* recover from a setback. This is explained more fully in chapter 10.

Just be patient and remember the following:

- Take a moment and take a breath.
- Remember Key Element #1 because you committed to making an effort, even during challenging times such as these.
- Give yourself a little time to collect your thoughts, because this person is important to you and you are focusing on your relationship and valuing the other person today (Key Element #2).
- Calmly reach out to them in some small way.
- Remind them that they are important to you and you want to get along, not fight, and be closer (Step #1). Do not focus on the topic; focus on the relationship.
- Reach out and say, "I'm sorry we had such a bad fight. I don't want to fight anymore" (Steps #1 and 3).
- Apologize for hurting them if they are upset, and assume responsibility. Be the person you want to be (Step #3).
- Regardless of whether they respond well or not, be respectful, thoughtful, and kind (Step #2). Stay with it.

Remember, this process *takes time*. Give yourselves credit for trying, and then go back to the RP. With practice, the conflicts won't last as long or be as intense, and/or one of you will begin to catch conflicts before they escalate. You learn to communicate and deal with conflicts by trusting each other with the skills to feel that you are really in this together.

Step #3: Example of Communicating Intentions with a Friend: "Please Just Let Me Talk"

Jim and Leah have been close friends for years. Jim is a more talkative, expressive person, and Leah is not as loquacious. It takes Leah a little longer than most people to express herself. When they are together, Leah often becomes frustrated with Jim because he tends to finish her sentences or he cuts her off midsentence.

Leah became very angry with Jim the last time they were together, when he once again interrupted her. As she was getting out of his car, she said angrily, "And I guess you know what I'm trying to say now too!" and she slammed the car door and walked away. Jim was shocked at her intensity and anger.

He immediately texted Leah asking, "What just happened? Why r u so mad?"

She didn't answer. He texted again and again, and still no response.

He called and got no answer. She didn't pick up her phone.

The next day he stopped by Leah's house and asked her why she had gotten so angry. He apologized for upsetting her, but was genuinely confused and now upset himself.

Leah then told him she was tired of him finishing her sentences and cutting her off. She said she was trying to tell him something that was important to her. When she was thinking about how to explain it to him, he jumped in as usual and assumed he knew what she was going to say. Leah told him she felt disrespected, because she was saying something that was important to her. She told him that, in fact, he was wrong about what he thought she was going to say. His impatience was a turnoff, and she was hurt and angry.

In this situation, the only thing Jim can do is apologize to his friend. He can tell Leah that he doesn't intentionally finish her sentences to hurt her feelings or make her angry with him (Step #3). He certainly is not doing it to be hurtful. He didn't know it bothered her that much, because she'd never said anything before now. He enjoys their friendship and wouldn't do anything to jeopardize it. He can promise to make an effort to be more thoughtful and not to finish her sentences in the future, and he hopes she accepts his apology.

Leah did accept his apology. She realized Jim wouldn't do anything to hurt her intentionally. She acknowledged that in this situation, the topic was something important to her, and she reacted strongly because she felt he was trivializing it.

From now on, while Jim is paying more attention to Leah while she is speaking, Leah's role is to tell Jim when she's annoyed at something. She agreed not to let things build to the point that she feels overwhelmed with emotion, acts out with tantrums, and leaves. Leah can also apologize for the way she handled that situation and promise to be a better communicator in the future.

Step #3: Example of Communicating Intentions between Parent and Child: "So I Am a Good Writer After All"

Ian, a high school student, asks his father to review an essay he wrote for one of his classes. His father reads the essay, and although he thinks it's well written, he marks it up with many corrections. Ian reacts badly when he sees all of his dad's corrections and feels hurt because he thought it was a great essay, one of his best.

They subsequently have a big argument in which Ian tells his father that he's always critical of him, which makes him feel frustrated and annoyed. He ends by saying he's never going to show his dad any more of his writing. His dad's immediate reaction is, "Then don't give it to me if you don't want me to correct it!"

Later in the day, Ian goes back to his father and explains, "I appreciate that you edited the essay for me, but I'm disappointed that you always find problems with my writing. It's frustrating, and it makes me feel like nothing's ever good enough for you."

"I'm sorry you're disappointed, Ian," his father says, "but I thought you wanted me to make corrections. I thought I was being helpful. My corrections are not to make you feel badly, but to show you how to make it better. I think you write very well. I like what you wrote, and my corrections are just minor things. I wasn't looking to be critical or make you feel badly. I'm sorry if I did, because I didn't mean to."

"OK," Ian replies. "Thanks."

Ian's dad was able to own his part in their interaction and apologize to his son, even though he never meant to say or do anything unkind. His corrections were not made to hurt Ian's feelings or to be overly critical, so he apologized for inadvertently hurting his son in the process (Step #3). The father recognized that in order to move forward, an apology was needed. He wanted Ian to see him as trying to be helpful, not critical, because this was never his intention.

"So far the changes are superficial. It's going to take time for me to trust again, but we're taking it one step at a time so neither of us gets hurt. So far, this RP is keeping it much calmer, which is great."

Chapter Seven

STEP #4: "I WILL GIVE YOU THE BENEFIT OF THE DOUBT."

STEP #4, the last step in plain English

"I will give you the benefit of the doubt."

Here is Step #4 in a nutshell: In Step #3, when the other person apologizes to you or acknowledges that something they said or did affected you negatively, it is imperative that you give something back to them in response.

Your role is to appreciate their apology, thank them, or at least acknowledge in some way that you are giving them the benefit of the doubt, also known as the "b of d." This means you acknowledge and believe (or want to believe) they did not intend to be hurtful toward you.

The Relationship Protocol takes both parties into account.

Both individuals in the relationship have a role and responsibility in the Relationship Protocol. In Step #4, the receiver of the apology has an important role in the interaction.

Letting go of hurt and pain starts here

The receiver of the apology acknowledges the apology, and

- appreciates that the other person acknowledged and recognized that they (the receiver) were upset;
- thanks the other person for apologizing;
- tells them they are giving them the benefit of the doubt; and
- makes an effort to let go of whatever upset them. They relinquish the hurt in an effort to continue moving forward together because the relationship is important to both of them.

Once the other person apologizes, your role, for the most part, is to give them the b of d. In other words, you are saying, "I believe you when you tell me you are sorry and that I am important to you" or "I believe you when you apologize for hurting me unintentionally about this situation or interaction."

The benefit of the doubt is used *only for one interaction* at a time.

Each time you give the other person the benefit of the doubt, you are giving it for that one interaction. Each interaction builds on the next, and this is how trust grows in your relationship, one step at a time. In the beginning of this process, you may have reservations about fully opening up and trusting or believing the other person. Just remember, according to the RP, the benefit of the doubt is not for the entire relationship or the person, but only for the particular interaction for which you are receiving an apology.

Therefore, if you don't fully trust the other person yet or fully believe in their apology, you are not being asked to grant them carte blanche trust or complete benefit of the doubt.

So, if you can, give them the benefit of the doubt for that one interaction. This is a crucial moment on your part because, in this final step, you are showing them that you, too, are making an effort toward change, willing to let things go, appreciating their efforts, and accepting their apology. Your job now is to make an effort to genuinely let go of your distress, upset, or anger for that interaction and allow change and trust to happen in your relationship.

The benefit of the doubt after an apology

When one person apologizes to another person and *if* they are given the benefit of the doubt, this demonstrates an acceptance of their apology and that the other person is now willing to move on. Here are two common examples:

- Haley demonstrates or expresses her unhappiness about something that her sister Zara has done. Zara apologizes to Haley for making her unhappy. Haley thanks Zara for apologizing, thus giving Zara the benefit of the doubt for her sincere apology.

- Zara notices that her comment or behavior seems to have hurt her sister Haley. Since Zara was not being intentionally hurtful, and she wants to get along better with Haley, Zara apologizes. Haley appreciates Zara's apology, and she gives her the benefit of the doubt.

The receiver of the apology, Haley, in this example, lets go of the offending words or action by relinquishing her need to hold onto the hurt. She believes in Zara's true intentions, simply because Zara said so.

By telling the other person that you are giving them the b of d, you are saying that you are beginning to trust them. You recognize that they are in this relationship with you. This shows your desire to get along and a willingness to let it go. The relationship can now move forward, one interaction at a time.

Think about how important it is to let go and be free of anger and hurt that may have been with you for years. It's dangerous if you keep holding on to it. Unless you can begin to let go of the wounds, hurts, and disappointments and find a new way to move forward, you will keep repeating the same pattern, and this cyclical pattern will essentially go nowhere.

Letting go also helps the other person to feel hopeful that things can be better in the future. They are more likely to respond in kind to your openness and your gesture of goodwill.

This final step can bring a big sigh of relief for both parties. It breaks the old tension. It shows that you are making an effort not to repeat the same harmful pattern over and over again. You are demonstrating a willingness to move to a better place together and restore hope for the future.

You have the power in that moment to break those destructive elements that have taken the enjoyment out of your relationship. This step opens up the possibility for a new, positive trajectory in your relationship.

Important note: The RP is an incremental trust-building process. The only way trust happens in relationships is if you start with the here and now, and begin a new way of communicating and building trust today. Old feelings, problems, and concerns can be addressed later, after you've established a healthier and more comfortable way of communicating.

Shift your priority to start making your relationship better.

To be successful using this model, you need to make your desire to improve your relationship more important than your need to hold onto past hurts. Invest in your future; don't hold onto the old toxic stuff. If you can, take it one interaction at a time. These interactions will ultimately build on each other.

Important times to give the benefit of the doubt

Sometimes you need to give the benefit of the doubt in order to move forward in your relationship. You may not want to, or you may find it difficult to do so, but without it, you won't build trust in your relationship.

For example, Joe tells Gail that he got home late because his boss called him into a meeting. Gail gives Joe the benefit of the doubt that he is being truthful. She does this because either Joe has never given her any reason to doubt him, or she decided to give him the b of d for this interaction alone, so they can begin building trust.

Step #4 can apply to many situations where there are longstanding issues. Do you think the other person

- is back to their old ways?
- doesn't have your back?
- isn't fully trustworthy?
- doesn't really care?
- isn't really trying to make things better?
- is doing something that creates doubt about their effort or integrity in the relationship?

Be aware that old issues, even ones that are completely valid, need to be put on the back burner, if possible, for now. You are not granting anyone full trust. However, if the other person seems genuinely sincere in their efforts, you want to try to give them the b of d—but again, only for that one time.

Step #4: Example of Giving the Benefit of the Doubt:
"Let's Get Past This"

Melissa: "I'm really upset that you didn't tell me about your next trip. I feel ignored, like I really don't matter to you."

Jake: "I genuinely forgot to tell you. I'm sorry. Please give me the benefit of the doubt that it was simply a mistake on my part."

The benefit of the doubt can be as simple as in this example. Jake apologized to Melissa immediately and asked her to give him the b of d so they can move past this hiccup in their relationship.

Step #4: Example of Giving the Benefit of the Doubt:
"Letting it Go"

"Lenny didn't react the way I'd hoped he would," Linda said. "He wasn't as excited for me about my new job. But this time, instead of getting upset with him and assuming his lack of reaction meant that he didn't care, I gave him the benefit of the doubt, and I chose to let it go. I avoided a potential conflict and decided to trust his intentions because I know that he does care."

In this example, Linda is giving the benefit of the doubt to Lenny, but she is not saying it out loud. This is perfectly fine because her actions demonstrate a mutual trust between them. Her choice was to give Lenny the benefit of the doubt because *she believes that he cares about her, and she trusts his intentions.* This concept doesn't always come naturally when first using the model, especially with difficult relationships. So, whenever possible, make an effort to give the b of d to help move things along and to avoid unnecessary and hurtful conflicts. Small steps, even baby steps, are OK as long as there's some movement in a positive direction.

How to give the benefit of the doubt

Here's are some options:

- You can make a conscious decision not to engage in negative thinking or assumptions about the other person's behavior, and instead trust their intentions and decide to give them the benefit of the doubt. (This is what Linda did in the previous example.)

- You can acknowledge in your own words that you notice the other person is making an effort. There's recognition or an understanding between you and the other person that you appreciate their effort or apology.

- You may want to simply say, "Thank you. I appreciate your apology."

- You can let them know that you not only appreciate their apology, but you are also going to give them the benefit of the doubt.

- Feel free to tell them, "When XXX occurred (earlier, recently, yesterday), I began to think about you as I used to before using the Relationship Protocol. I thought you weren't really making an effort, but I want to give you the benefit of the doubt now. I also want this to work, and I do notice some effort on your part." This is helpful in situations where trust was lacking and a new relationship is forming. These statements encourage and motivate the other person to continue making an effort. If there is no acknowledgment on your part, in time they may stop making an effort believing nothing they do matters.

There is no pressure to give someone the benefit of the doubt when you are not ready to do so. If this is your situation, it's best to be honest. Respectfully tell them that even though you appreciate their efforts, at this time it's hard for you to give them the b of d, but you hope to or might be able to do so in the future. While you are not currently able to give them what they may want from you, you are at least being respectful and giving them some hope for the future.

This kind of encouragement can inject hope and motivation and can move the trust meter up a notch. This is important throughout your relationship. As trust grows, the benefit of the doubt can come much more naturally and more often.

- You could say, "I'm trying to give you the benefit of the doubt. I'm doing my best for now. I want to trust you, but I'm just not ready yet" or "While I don't fully trust you today, I hope I can in the future."

- If you don't want to acknowledge the other person's effort verbally, simply interact with them in a more positive and open way. Most likely, it will become obvious that you are indirectly giving them the b of d. Going forward, try to communicate at some point that you support their effort.

Step #4: Example of Giving the Benefit of the Doubt, Stepdaughter to Stepmother: Evil Stepmother...or Not

"I want to give my stepmother the b of d, but she's a difficult person. She's done some crummy things to my sister and me in the past, and although we were much younger then, those feelings sometimes still come back when I'm around her. Lately, she's been nicer to me, and when I lost my job last winter, she offered to let me move back home. It would be hard to move back there, since I've been on my own for a while now, but I might need to live there for financial reasons. It would mean a lot to my dad if my stepmom and I got along, because he and I are still close. I'm just not sure how to start that process—or if I want to."

In this situation, there's a negative history of mistrust and hurt. Clearly this person is not going to jump in and trust her stepmother's intentions, nor should she. In all situations, as in this one, you offer the benefit of the doubt for that one interaction or situation. Take the situation incrementally—one day, one step at a time—until there's evidence that the person is in fact worthy of your trust with no ulterior motive. At that point, you may be able to begin trusting their intentions. You will know when you have arrived at that place, if ever.

This person may ultimately want to have a pleasant and more positive relationship with their stepmother, but they do not have to confide intimate secrets to her or become best friends. That may not be an option, and that needs to be OK.

When you should or should not give the benefit of the doubt

You may have valid reasons to be hesitant or not to trust someone. What if you don't trust the other person's efforts, or you continue to be critical of their behavior, seeing it through a negative lens? For now, if you are going to use the Relationship Protocol effectively, you need to be aware of your own fixed, negative perspective, whether valid or not. It is your responsibility to try to put it aside, if possible, in an attempt to be more open to the other person's sincere efforts. If you can, the goal is to gradually remove the negative lens and increasingly give the b of d because they have shown that they are trustworthy over time.

If you are cynical or resentful about the other person because of your history, you will most likely be closed off and unwilling to notice even small efforts they are making. If this is the case, remember that you are only giving them the b of d for that one apology today. Make an effort to take each interaction one small step at a time as you begin to build trust.

Step #4: Example of How Small Fibs Lead to Lack of Trust: "But I Only Lied a Little"

In some relationships, one person decides to tell a white lie because the truth is going to get them in trouble or disappoint the other person. For whatever reason, they choose not to be completely honest. This occurs in many relationships.

127

Roommate #1 to Roommate #2: "Did you pay the phone bill? It was overdue, and they're threatening to disconnect."

Roommate #2: "Yes." (But, in fact, he didn't. His answer is just to placate his roommate so he will stop asking questions.)

When or if the phone does get turned off, Roommate #2 is now caught in a lie. He may think it's a small one, not worthy of a big reaction from his roommate. However, any intentional lie is breaking trust and is considered intentionally hurtful. White lies add up, and even one white lie often results in an inability to give the person who told the lie the benefit of the doubt.

In close relationships with family, roommates, romantic partners, or at work, we want to give those around us the benefit of the doubt. One lie, or even a small fib just to avoid a conflict, can squash all the trust that has been built between you and the other person, and justifiably make the other person question your trustworthiness.

Think before you utter a white lie, and be prepared for the repercussions if you get caught. A lie is a lie. It feels like a betrayal, and it erodes trust. If you are dishonest, don't get upset when the other person doesn't grant you the benefit of the doubt, because you haven't done anything to earn that gift.

Let the Relationship Protocol help you find clarity about yourself and your relationships.

For now, it is not critical that you like or even trust everything about the other person. You can still have a relationship with someone and not want to be fully invested in all aspects. If you follow the model, take the benefit of the doubt incrementally, and let it build. It will help you to begin to see the possibilities as well as the limitations of the relationship.

Unfortunately, there are situations where people may not deserve the benefit of the doubt:

- When someone is a repeat offender who continually does things that are untrustworthy, offensive, intentionally hurtful, and betrays your trust.

- When someone's words repeatedly don't line up with their actions—they say one thing but do another—it leads to confusion and mistrust. It is difficult to give someone the b of d when words and actions are not in sync. This behavior is usually a warning to be more cautious and take things slowly.

- When there is a clear issue of betrayal or mistrust, yet the other person never takes responsibility and even vehemently defends their actions or casts blame on others or on you, this is a major red flag. In those circumstances, deflecting or not being open demonstrates an inability to be truthful.

You have the option of telling the other person that you are not giving them the b of d now, or possibly ever. You can also consider giving them the benefit of the doubt in the future if they change their behavior. If this is the case, trust may begin to build over time, but slowly and taking each interaction one at a time.

You don't have to withhold giving someone the b of d completely; consider starting small and letting it grow naturally as your relationship grows. Notice if their behavior matches their words. And don't believe everything someone tells you until they have shown themselves by their actions to be trustworthy and consistent over time.

Time is the telltale sign of a change in behavior in each of these situations. But keep in mind that you give the b of d for each separate interaction. They may deserve the benefit of the doubt in certain circumstances, but not in others. Pay attention to see if each interaction builds on the next. If this doesn't happen, you'll then have more clarity as to why the person should not be trusted.

If the other person has broken trust in the past and is behaving secretively or there is no transparency, talk to them about your concerns. You may see them as a trustworthy person, but you also may feel they might be hiding things from you. Use the RP to address your concerns. Don't put them on the defensive or alienate them, but don't avoid talking about your concerns either. Communicating and being open, transparent, and respectful can go a long way to rebuild trust. Without these, you will find it difficult to give the other person the benefit of the doubt.

Step #4: Example of Not Giving the Benefit of the Doubt:
"No Honesty, No B of D"

In this example, the wife has had serious problems with a drug addiction and has repeatedly lied about her whereabouts and her drug usage. She's upset with her husband because he won't give her the benefit of the doubt. He uses the Relationship Protocol model to discuss his inability to trust her behavior.

Husband to wife: "I love you, but you aren't trustworthy. You lied to me again about taking those pills. I can't give you the benefit of the doubt and just go on as if nothing happened. Trust my intentions and give me the benefit of the doubt that I'm not saying this to be mean or hurtful. But your own actions have rendered you untrustworthy, and therefore, I can't give you the b of d yet. If you become more open with me and continue to go for help, I will want to give you the b of d. But you need to start being more transparent and upfront. Trust takes time. Let's see how it goes. I'm not making any promises."

The husband is using the entire RP model to talk about a topic that is very important, intense, and deeply upsetting to both of them. He is kind and direct with his wife about how her dishonest behavior has made it impossible for him to trust her and give her the benefit of the doubt. He asked his wife to trust his intentions and give him the b of d that he is not just being mean, but for now, he is concerned and taking a strong stand. He spoke respectfully and reassuringly but was also calm, firm, and honest.

So *you've* been untrustworthy

Your apology may not be accepted. The other person may say something like, "Great, you apologized. You can keep apologizing, but it doesn't necessarily mean anything!" Or they may simply say, "No, thanks, I don't accept your apology."

This is not unusual, especially when there is a history of hurt and frustration. Be prepared that they may not fully accept your apology at this moment, even though you are being sincere.

Instead, before apologizing, think ahead about how you might respond respectfully and thoughtfully—not angrily—if they do reject your apology. Also, try to lower your expectations to reduce your disappointment. Then stop and hit the pause button, take a deep breath, and think about an appropriate answer before responding.

Keep in mind that if you fight back or answer them with anger or defensiveness, the old negative cycle continues on, and you've only increased the distance between you. However, if you are more thoughtful in your responses, trust building can start with you.

Important note: This is the first test of your commitment to making an effort (Key Element #1), so don't get discouraged or annoyed or give up. Remember, talk is cheap, and the other person wants to see that, from now on, your actions follow your words. This is a process.

Here are some suggestions about how to approach or respond to them:

- "Jennifer, I understand why it's hard for you to give me the benefit of the doubt this time, but I do want you to trust me again." (Validating their feelings helps.)

- "I do sincerely apologize, and I'm going to keep trying."
- "I feel badly that you can't give me the benefit of the doubt, Ruta, and I don't understand why, but I'm not giving up on our relationship."

If you are honest in your desire to better both yourself and the relationship, then let time be your friend. Stay with it, don't give up, and eventually the other person will see that you are sincere and making an honest effort to work things out. Time is a key variable when you're making an effort, especially when there's a difficult history to overcome.

Change begins with you

When you continue to repeat old patterns and use behaviors that negatively affect your relationship, expect your relationship to suffer. The old adage about insanity from Albert Einstein works here: "Doing the same thing over and over again and expecting a different result—that is the definition of insanity."

You are only responsible for yourself, and you have an obligation to yourself to be the best person you can be. Are there things you need to work on or change in order to be a better communicator?

Also, if you are quiet or have difficulty communicating, the other person may not give you the benefit of the doubt, because they do not fully understand what is happening for you, your feelings, your circumstances, and so on. It behooves you to find a way to offer some information that may help others to better understand, feel closer to you, and ultimately give you the b of d.

Jumping to conclusions

Do you make negative assumptions about the meaning of someone's behavior? When someone does something that hurts your feelings, do you quickly assume you know what they meant by it and react accordingly without asking them to explain?

Jumping to conclusions usually does more harm than good, especially if you don't trust the other person's intentions (Step #3) and can't comfortably give them the b of d (Step #4). You will probably negatively skew the reason for their behavior. But ask yourself, why do I make assumptions about someone else's behavior without checking in? Think about giving them the b of d for now, until you can gather more information.

Suggestion: Instead of jumping to negative conclusions and getting upset, calmly and respectfully ask the other person about it. Both of you will feel better if you can talk without accusation and assumptions. Approach them by giving them the benefit of the doubt and being open to hearing them explain, because your initial reaction may be incorrect. If you focus more on who *you* want to be in this relationship, you may see results more quickly.

Here's a common example of an assumption: Your boss asks you to stay late to finish the report that's due Monday. You spend the rest of the day worrying that he's upset with you and you may get fired. At the end of the day, he expresses his appreciation for your help with the report and thanks you for being such a hard worker. You breathe a sigh of a relief!

Please hold your thought

When the other person mentions something that is bothering them during a conversation, it is important to wait until their issue is fully addressed before you bring up your issues or another one in response. Let the RP model run its course completely on the topic you're discussing, with them trusting your intentions and giving you the b of d.

It's best to follow this guideline:

Before you start another topic or jump in with a defensive comment or retort, take a moment to let that first topic finish, as if it is now tied in a neat package, before you move on and add something new or change the topic. You might even want to check in and respectfully ask if that topic is complete, because you also have something you'd like to discuss.

This is not point-counterpoint or a competition to be right. By listening and allowing the first part of the discussion (their part) to finish, you are being respectful of whatever they wanted to talk about, not ratcheting things up or fueling the conflict. You are simply pointing out something that is bothering you when they are finished speaking about their topic. You will find more on this topic in the section called "Me too interactions" in chapter 9.

Call it a misfire

A misfire is when the other person genuinely misinterprets something you've said or done, usually in a negative way. Instead of going back and forth trying to convince them of your innocence or trying to rewind the conversation to explain how they are incorrect, just label it a "misfire" between the two of you and try to move on. Use Step #4, the benefit of the doubt, to show them you had good intentions and aren't just making excuses. This should not be used if you are being dishonest in some way or are trying to manipulate the other person. This is to help build trust, avoid conflicts, and move things along in a positive way.

Here's how it works: Let the other person know that they misunderstood what you were saying or doing. Then ask them to give you the benefit of the doubt and tell them it simply was a misfire between the two of you. You are essentially saying, "No one is at fault. I genuinely want to get along with you, but something about that situation or interaction misfired and didn't go well." In that moment, you are asking them to trust your intentions. If they are willing to chalk it up to a misunderstanding, you just defused a potential conflict before it had a chance to build. If necessary, apologize for the misfire, as it was unintentional, so the relationship can get back on track. Either way, this is an opportunity to defuse a situation quickly and build some trust.

Use a cue word to stop conflicts in the future.

Saying the word *misfire* alone or in a sentence or two, such as "*I think we just had a misfire. Please give me the benefit of the doubt that this was just a misunderstanding,*" shows that you care and are taking control to prevent a possible fight. You can also plan to use the word *misfire* or another neutral or fun cue word in your own relationship when these kinds of interactions occur between the two of you.

Examples of Misfires

Wife: "I wish we had a system for paying bills so I could understand more about our finances."

Husband: "Are you accusing me of not handling our finances properly? I take offense to that."

The wife can immediately address her husband's comments by apologizing for offending him and then explain that it was a misfire. She can clarify that her comment was about her lack of understanding about their finances, not an insult about him. He gives her the benefit of the doubt.

One person says in all sincerity, "I love you and I want to be with you, but I can't fully change who I am, and I may not be enough for you." The other person hears this as a threat and gets angry and defensive.

It is up to the person who made the comment to stop the action and label their discussion as a misfire, a misinterpretation, before this interaction about a sensitive topic escalates. The person needs to apologize because he or she did not intend to be hurtful, but was simply being honest and respectful about a difficult subject.

One partner decides to go to sleep early because he is exhausted. The other partner interprets this atypical behavior as his way of dodging spending time with her. In fact, the person going to bed early is just tired, not avoiding anything. Label it as a misfire, apologize for the misunderstanding, and give each other the b of d.

That's not what I *meant* to write: texting, e-mails, and the written word

Communication is occurring more and more via writing that is not in person or face-to-face. Written communication, such as texts, e-mails, and social media exchanges, gives you time to think before responding, and it doesn't necessarily prepare you for dealing with what's happening in real time, in that moment, without delay. Using the RP model and learning new communication tools, such as how to observe and connect with what's going on between you and the other person, are important life skills.

Many people in relationships speak to each other primarily by texting or other methods that aren't face-to-face. When you rely on the written word only, there are no visual cues; everything that is said is open to interpretation. There are no facial expressions, body language signals, or other behaviors to observe, and you don't get the benefit of hearing the tone, attitude, or volume of the other person's voice. This form of communication is the essence of giving the benefit of the doubt. You are inherently trusting that you both understand the true meaning of what is being communicated.

STEP #4: "I WILL GIVE YOU THE BENEFIT OF THE DOUBT."

If you know the other person well and your communication is typically more natural and easy, misinterpretations are less likely. It is expected that you will give the other person the b of d, and it's unstated, given without question. Yet in other relationships and at different times, when relying only on non-face-to-face communication, there is the potential for more misunderstandings. Many of these misfires concern questioning the b of d and trusting each other's intentions. Because there are fewer cues with the written word, giving the other person the b of d comes into question more often.

If you are unsure about the attitude or tone in something you are sent and it seems negative to you, you may need to ask the sender for clarification. Don't jump to conclusions; ask them a question instead of assuming your negative interpretation is correct. The other person can then explain what they meant to say, and hopefully the conversation can move along.

Communication is simplest to read when it's face-to-face. When you can see the other person in front of you, you can pick up cues from their body language and facial expressions as well as listen for tone, volume, and attitude. Talking on the telephone is better than written communication, but adding the visual component of face-to-face interaction often decreases the odds of misinterpretation. Regardless of your form of communication, when you are doubtful or confused about the meaning of the message you received, ask for clarification, and then think about giving the benefit of the doubt.

Step #4: Example of When Text Messages Are Misunderstood: "Don't Bother"

A couple's daughter is receiving an award that night at the high school auditorium. The husband is running late from work and texts his wife to ask if he can meet her at the high school. He knows she doesn't like walking into these events alone, but it can't be helped because his work schedule dictates when he can leave the office.

Gavin: Can we just meet at the HS? If I pick u up, we'll be even later, but I'll come by and get u if u want me 2.

Alison: Don't bother. I'll meet u there.

Gavin: I've had a long day. Pls don't give me a hard time.

Alison: What r u talking abt? I'm not giving u hard time.

Gavin: I can tell ur annoyed with the 'don't bother.' Knock it off pls… I'll get there as soon as I can.

Alison: Pls don't come if ur in a bad mood!

In this example, Gavin assumed his wife might be upset that he was running late, because he knows she doesn't like walking into these types of events alone. He interpreted her "don't bother" as having an angry or annoyed tone. Alison, on the other hand, seems to be saying, "Don't bother picking me up. We'll just meet there." without a negative attitude. Because he has had similar experiences in the past when his wife has been annoyed, they may have a tougher time resolving this problem via text. Gavin's tardiness is just another layer of stress for him. Going forward, Alison could send Gavin a text saying, "Pls give me the b of d, I'm not annoyed," or Gavin could check in without jumping to a negative conclusion.

Because they're going to see each other and have an opportunity to resolve the matter in person, the best thing for them to do is quickly acknowledge the misunderstanding and make an effort to enjoy the evening. Alison can address the issue immediately upon her husband's arrival by suggesting that he misunderstood her and that she is not annoyed, but glad he was coming to the awards ceremony. Gavin can then apologize for assuming she was upset and explain that he was overwhelmed at work and not in a great mood to start. They trust each other's intentions (Step #3) and give each other the b of d (Step #4), and voila, it's over. It can be that simple if both sides cooperate and let the misfire go.

Step #4: Example of Giving the Benefit of the Doubt Instead of Jumping to Conclusions: "Assume and Then React Accordingly"

Do you frequently take things personally, even when the situation has little or nothing to do with you? Do you automatically, and therefore quickly, jump to conclusions? The following three interactions address different topics but with the same theme. This is a common response that many people have with the important people in their life.

In each example, one person makes assumptions and judgments about the meaning of another person's behavior. And by the way, in each of these examples, the person making the assumptions is wrong.

Jillian: "You never ask me, 'How was your day?'"

Her mother, Stephanie: "I guess that's true. When we all come home, we just start talking about other things."

Jillian: "You don't ask me, but you always ask Zach how his day was. If you notice, you rarely ever ask me. I think you really don't care about anyone except Zachary. I'm tired of things always being about him."

Stephanie (appears surprised by her daughter's reaction, because she really does care about her daughter and her day): "I'm sorry you think I don't ask you because I don't care. That is not true at all. I care a lot about you, and of course I am always interested in your day. Your brother's been having a tough time in school lately, so I guess I'm more inclined to ask him. I didn't mean for you to feel slighted, and I'm sorry if I hurt your feelings. I'll try to be better about it." *(Using Steps #1, #2, and #3)*

Jillian: "OK." *(Step #4)*

Stephanie: "So, how was your day today?"

Jillian: "Nothing's really going on. I just like it when you ask!"

Diane to her girlfriend Lisa: "I realized today that you don't want to spend time with me. It's OK if you don't want to hang out."

Lisa: "What are you talking about?"

Diane: "We've talked about going on a girls weekend together, and I've asked you many times. You keep avoiding the subject. Lately, you never want to do anything. You're always too busy."

Lisa starts to get angry but stops herself because she realizes that somehow she's hurt her friend's feelings unintentionally. Diane isn't saying this to give her a hard time or to make her angry. (Step #3): "First of all, I thought we talked about not planning anything now because there's just too much going on in my life right now. You know how busy I've been, and I am certainly not avoiding you. I'm just busy. I promise."

Diane: "Are you mad at me for telling you I was upset with you?"

Lisa: "I'm not mad, and I don't want to hurt your feelings. I'm sorry if I made you feel that way, but I think you're reading into something that isn't there. I would like a girls weekend, but just not now." (Steps #1, #2, and #3)

Diane: "OK. Well, I'm glad I told you, and I'm glad I was wrong." (Step 4)

Husband: "If you don't want to be intimate with me, just tell me. You keep falling asleep in the kids' room, and it's really annoying. I'm tired of asking you to have sex."

Wife: "I'm sorry if my falling asleep in their room makes you feel hurt or rejected, but it's not on purpose. Why would you think that I don't want to be intimate with you? I promise, I don't plan it. I hope you believe me." (Steps #1, #2, and #3. Also, intimacy is a sensitive subject, so be extra kind when discussing this topic.)

Husband: "Yes, I believe you. I'm glad I brought it up because, honestly, I've been really angry with you about this." (Step #4)

Wife: "I wish you would've brought it up sooner. Why don't we plan to have a night together this weekend?"

In the three examples above, one person made a value judgment about the other person's behavior. They each decided and concluded that the other person's behavior meant something negative. They assumed that the other person didn't care, didn't want to spend time with them, and in the last example, were intentionally avoiding having sex.

Here's the key part: One person made an assumption about the other person's behavior and then reacted accordingly. Each person felt hurt or angry without checking in to see if their assumptions were accurate. They did not give the other person the benefit of the doubt or trust their intentions. Each offered assumptions as if they knew their assumptions to be true and valid. They also did not communicate using Steps #1 and #2.

Key point: If they didn't eventually check in with the other person to see if their conclusions were correct, who knows how long they would have made incorrect assumptions, reacted based on incorrect information, and built up resentment in their own mind.

People often jump to conclusions without the courtesy of asking the other person what they meant. When this occurs in relationships, it can be destructive and toxic, especially if it happens often or if it builds up over time. In the examples above, none of the three individuals trusted the other person's intentions, and they didn't give them the b of d. The next time you have a question about why someone close to you is doing something you don't like or about one of their behaviors that makes you uncomfortable, don't assume there's a negative reason. Instead, thoughtfully ask them about it, which will be easier to do if you are using the Relationship Protocol.

Step #4: Example of Giving a Friend the Benefit of the Doubt:
"Is She Just Using Me?"

Kathie: "My friend Bobbie isn't my friend anymore because she's a user. I get really ticked off when I think of what a user she is."

Judy: "Why? What did she do?"

Kathie: "She liked hanging out with me when I had an apartment near her office, but now that I've moved, I never hear from her. She's too busy for me now, so I don't consider her a friend anymore."

Judy: "Have you called her? Have you told her that you're upset with her or that you miss hanging out with her?"

Kathie: "No. Why would I?"

Judy: "Because you're assuming she used you, rather than thinking that she just may be busy or preoccupied with something else in her life. Why would you assume she isn't interested in your friendship? Did she indicate that in any other way?"

Kathie: "No, I guess not, but I haven't heard from her since I moved."

Judy: "Maybe you're just hurt. That makes more sense to me than being ticked off and throwing away a friendship. Call Bobbie and see if she's free to get together. If you want, tell her you're hurt, or just enjoy her company and make an effort to see her more often. Don't automatically assume she doesn't want to be your friend or she's using you because you haven't heard from her. That sounds like some insecurities on your part and possibly a big stretch."

In this example, as in the examples before, Kathie jumped to conclusions and made her own interpretation that her friend

Bobbie didn't want to be her friend and had been using her because she had not been in contact. Kathie didn't trust Bobbie's intentions (Step #3) or give her the b of d (Step #4). She jumped to conclusions about what Bobbie's lack of contact actually meant.

Step #4: Example of a Mother and Daughter: "Mother, Why are You Always So Critical of Me?"

The interaction in this example is common, and occurs frequently in many kinds of relationships. This dynamic exists when one person believes that the other person is being negative and criticizing them whenever they say anything.

Mother: "*Emily, why do you think that everything I say to you is negative?*"

Emily: "*Because you always say things to me with a negative or critical tone. I'm beginning to think I can't do anything right in your eyes.*"

Mother: "*That is absolutely not true! For some reason, you seem to hear it that way, but it's not true.*"

Emily: "*You just made a comment about my clothes, and earlier you said something about my weight. I get tired of it.*"

Mother: "*I said your shirt was creased. Is that a crime? And I don't remember saying anything about your weight. I know not to say anything, because I don't want you to get mad at me. Whenever I say even the most benign things, they get turned around in your head. I think you are terrific. I don't think of you negatively, and I'm not sure how to change that thinking*"

146

on your part. But honestly, it's very hurtful to me that you see me as always being negative when I'm really not."

In this example, both people need to stop and use the Relationship Protocol before their conversation gets any worse. Emily is not trusting her mother's intentions or giving her the benefit of the doubt. They might want to plan so that the next time Emily feels badly or her mother notices Emily recoiling or getting upset, they do something differently.

After the RP: If Emily's mother notices an unexpected reaction from her, she will immediately ask Emily, "What happened?" On the other side, if Emily knows she's reacting badly to her mother's comment, she will point it out to her mother in that moment or soon thereafter in a respectful way. This will give her mother an opportunity to say that she didn't intend her comment in a negative way (Step #1). Emily can trust her mother's intentions, give her the b of d (Step #4), and hopefully move on.

Emily can do this each time she feels that a comment has a negative flavor. After a period of time, Emily and her mother may begin to notice why she reacts so strongly. It may reveal if her mother's tone or her own insecurities are the culprit—or both. If they work on it together, trusting each other's intentions (Step #3) and giving the b of d (Step #4), they have a great shot at improving their communication.

Step #4: Example of Giving Benefit of the Doubt
Making an Effort: "Can You Please Tone It Down?!"

Barbara: "I understand your therapist told you to tell me how you're feeling about our relationship, but she obviously didn't tell you how to talk to me about it. You came on so strong, and you got really loud, which made me tune out. Anyone would get angry and defensive if they were spoken to like that. Instead—and please hear me—I want to know when you're upset with me, but please think ahead about what and how you're going to talk to me. I'll listen if you speak nicer to me. I want to get along with you too. I'm glad you're trying to communicate with me."

Joan: "This is hard for me. I don't have it all together yet, but I am trying. Please give me the benefit of the doubt. I'll try to think ahead and be calmer when I talk to you about something that upsets me. I just want us to be close like we were when we were younger."

Barbara: "I want that, too, but you can't come at me like gangbusters—it's a turnoff. Let's put this behind us. I'm glad we talked."

Joan: "Me, too, and thanks!"

In this example, Barbara reassured Joan that she wants her to tell her when she's upset, but not in the way she's been communicating. She used Step #1, "I want to get along with you." She also used many "I" sentences to lessen her sister's possible defensiveness. She told Joan that the message wasn't what was wrong, but *how* she communicated needed a shift. The tone and volume of her voice was too strong. Barbara was more effective because she spoke to her in a positive and constructive way, effectively communicating how she felt. Joan was also able to express her desire to have a better relationship with her sister. This is a good start all around.

If Joan thinks ahead about how she will communicate with Barbara when things upset her, and if they both continue to be patient and understanding, they can have productive conversations about tough subjects in the future. The benefit of the doubt will build with each interaction. When Joan shows gratitude for Barbara's patience and asks for her to give her the b of d (Step #4), this helps them to start building trust. Hopefulness increases as their relationship grows, because each person feels supported and valued. They also both tolerated the conversation and expressed their desire to improve their relationship.

The good news is that positive communication feels good. The positives can build quickly and replace the old negative patterns. The shift in your thinking may be subtle, like turning the dial one notch, but it can make a huge difference for both of you after being stuck for so long.

Step #4: Example of Giving a Friend the Benefit of the Doubt:
"I'm Worried about You"

Karen is concerned that her friend Donna is drinking too much and may have a drinking problem. She wants to speak to Donna about this issue but is concerned about making her angry. Donna is known among their friends as someone who can be defensive and doesn't take feedback well.

Karen: "You are one of my best friends. The last thing I want to do is upset you or make you mad at me, but I have to say something to you because this is important. I'm really worried that lately you've been drinking a lot. I know six months ago our friends tried to do an intervention, and they also spoke to you about this. You've blacked out three times that I know of in the last two months, and you don't remember anything that happened. Can you understand where I'm coming from and why I'm bringing it up? I'm worried, and I do think you have a drinking problem. I will go with you to AA, if you're willing to give it a shot."

Donna (annoyed): "First of all, I don't have a drinking problem, and I don't remember any intervention. I know you care about me, but you don't have to worry. I'm fine."

Karen: "Please don't be mad at me. Just think about what I'm saying, and trust that I'm your friend and I care. I'm not saying these things to be mean, but your behavior is not cool; it's very risky and unsafe. About six months ago, didn't Kaitlyn, Valerie, and Bridget talk to you about their concerns? We don't want anything to happen to you, and that's the only reason I'm saying something now."

Donna: "OK, I do appreciate you coming to me with this, and while I'm not happy hearing that you guys are worried about me, I will try to tone it down. If I can't, then I'll consider going to a meeting, but I think I can do it myself."

In this example, Karen spoke to Donna with kindness (Step #2) and asked Donna to trust her intentions (Step #3) as her friend. In the end, Donna did seem to trust Karen, and she gave her the benefit of the doubt (Step #4), even if she didn't fully agree with Karen's assessment of her drinking habits. This may be the first of many conversations on this topic between these friends. Donna probably responded much better than Karen expected, so that's a good start.

This situation is serious in that Donna is demonstrating unsafe behaviors that must change. Karen was able to speak about this serious matter in a supportive and compassionate way (Step #2). It is now up to Donna to change her drinking habits or reconcile the fact that she may have a drinking problem. If she doesn't change her ways, her friends cannot give her the b of d or trust her intentions (Steps #3 and #4).

Step # 4: Example of Giving the Benefit of the Doubt between Parent and Child: "Are You Getting a New Boyfriend Anytime Soon?"

Corrinne is an eighteen-year-old girl with a boyfriend whom her parents don't seem to like. They told Corrinne that they wished she were with someone who was more communicative and would talk more with them when he comes to the house. Her parents have recently been using the RP, and according to Corrinne, they have changed how they talk to her about the "boyfriend situation." For example:

Before RP: Ellen, Corrinne's mother: "Corrinne, when are you going to get a new boyfriend? He's nice, but Dad and I think you can do better. Don't you? Be with someone who comes into the house and talks to us. We don't even know him. He doesn't talk at all. Does he even talk to you?"

Now using RP: Ellen: "Corrinne, I know you've said you're happy in your relationship, and Dad and I are glad you're happy. We would just like to try to get to know your boyfriend better. Would you consider inviting him to the house for dinner so we could spend a little time with him? It's uncomfortable for us that you're out with a boy we don't know. Can you understand that we trust you, but we just don't know him at all?"

In this example, Ellen originally was direct in expressing strong negative feelings about her daughter's boyfriend without any regard for how Corrinne might feel about him. This approach was off-putting to Corrinne.

When Ellen began using the RP, she spoke to her daughter in a caring way about a sensitive topic (Step #2). Ellen didn't criticize the boyfriend, but instead asked Corrinne to try to understand the situation from her perspective. In this example, Corrinne's mother spoke kindly (Step #2), giving Corrinne the benefit of the doubt (Step #3) by telling Corrinne she trusts her and asking her to consider her parents' feelings as well. This new approach made it easier for Corrinne to cooperate and comply with her mother's request.

Step #4: Example of a New Relationship, Getting to Know Each Other: "Tell Me Again—Why Are You Snooping?"

Sierra reported seeing her boyfriend of six months going into her backpack without her permission when she wasn't in the room. Until that moment, she completely trusted him, but that behavior made her question his integrity. She wondered why he was suspicious of her and checking through her things. Was he looking for something specific, or was he stealing money from her? Her mind started racing, but before she got too involved in getting angry and concerned, she decided to ask him directly.

Sierra: "I want to know why you went into my backpack earlier. It makes me uncomfortable, because you didn't ask me first and I wouldn't go into your things. I don't like people going through my things without permission. I'm not saying I don't trust you, George, but can you understand how I feel?"

George: "Yes, I get it. I'm sorry. I didn't mean anything by it. I needed some singles to pay the tip for the pizza. I thought it would be OK to check ahead of time, and I'm sorry if it bothered you."

Sierra: "OK, but in the future, please ask me first. And thanks for understanding."

In the example, this relatively new couple is still learning about each other and building trust. It's a very good sign that Sierra's boyfriend didn't get defensive or react negatively to her questions about him going into her backpack. George doesn't seem to be hiding anything, and he understands, given the newness of their relationship, why she might question his behavior. He, in essence, gave Sierra the benefit of the doubt, and he trusted her intentions, her reasons for asking him (Step #3 and #4). Sierra also gave George the benefit of the doubt that it was an innocent act (Step #4). Now she can store this information in the back of her mind as they get to know each other better.

We give others the b of d gradually over time. If, in time, Sierra sees that her boyfriend is trustworthy, she will continue to give him the b of d, and eventually, they may have a long-term, healthy, trusting relationship. If, however, other things occur that make her doubt his intentions or trustworthiness, then a different conversation will most likely take place between them.

THE RELATIONSHIP PROTOCOL

Using Steps #3 and #4 together:

What to do when you or the other person is unhappy

"I will never intentionally hurt you."
"I will give you the benefit of the doubt."

There are many variations of how Steps #3 and #4 come into play. Below are the most basic ways for how they can and should be used in your relationships. If they seem too perfect or unrealistic, keep reading, because there's more information about the many ways of implementing this model.

A gentle reminder brings the relationship into focus.

Suggestion: When either of you approaches the other to talk about something that is bothering you, in the beginning why not start with **"I want to talk to you. Let's pay attention and use the RP."** A reminder to use the model increases your odds of a better outcome, because both of you are prompted ahead of time to be aware and pay close attention during that interaction.

When you notice that the other person is unhappy

A. You observe that they appear to be angry, sad, quiet, etc.

B. Immediately stop whatever you're saying or doing and ask them about your observation. Your priority is to check in with them, not to continue whatever you were saying or doing. "Are you upset? Did I do something to upset you?" (Step #3)

C. Hopefully they tell you if something is bothering them. They may say you did or said something that made them mad.

D. You respond, "I'm sorry that I made you mad (consider repeating the word they used). I certainly didn't do it on purpose. It wasn't intentional." (Step #3)

E. When they accept your apology, they are giving you the benefit of the doubt that you want to get along and not intentionally make them mad. (Step #4)

The toughest parts of Step #3 are stopping yourself as soon as you notice a potential problem brewing and then sincerely apologizing when they tell you what's bothering them. Because your intention is never to be hurtful, the apologetic response is always better in that moment than defending yourself, proving that they are wrong, or getting upset at them.

When you don't overreact when they tell you what's wrong, you are making a strong statement that you appreciate them, their reaction (feelings), and your relationship (Key Element #2). This powerful component defuses conflicts and quickly changes the way you relate to one another. However, keep in mind that Steps #3 and #4 will never happen unless you are paying attention to yourself and the other person.

When you are unhappy

A. You are not pleased at something that the other person said or did, and you are upset.

B. As soon as you are able, calmly and thoughtfully tell the other person, "When you said/did XXX, I felt like you were being XXX to me." You can add that you don't think they said or did it to be hurtful, but regardless, it bothered you. (You are telling them upfront that you are giving them the b of d.)

C. They then apologize for coming across sounding XXX because that wasn't their intention. The last thing they want to do is hurt you, so they apologize. (Step #3)

D. You thank them for apologizing. You can add that you believe they didn't do it on purpose because you know they also have also been trying to make things better. (You are giving them the b of d, Step #4.)

In this scenario, the toughest parts can be figuring out how to tell the other person that you are bothered by something they did and then giving them the b of d, accepting their apology.

Remember to address the issue at a time that's good for both of you, and bring up your feelings thoughtfully, not in an accusatory tone. It's now your role to accept the apology, trust their intentions, and give them the benefit of the doubt for *this* interaction. It is hoped that you can let go of your negative feelings after the apology so you can move forward together.

The benefit of giving the benefit of the doubt

When the ultimate goal is to improve a close relationship, give the benefit of the doubt whenever possible so you can keep the momentum going with each experience.

Give the benefit of the doubt for all of the Relationship Protocol.

One of the best ways to optimize your success with this program is to give the other person the benefit of the doubt for *all* of the Relationship Protocol Key Elements and Steps.

This *is how individuals in healthy relationships naturally think of the other person.* They relate to and communicate with one another by inherently giving them the b of d. This is an integral part of healthy communication.

Important note: Think about your close relationships. Hopefully there's at least one person in your life, perhaps a parent, sibling or child, that you are committed to having a good relationship with, and they know without question, that they are important to you. Of course, (think of the RP) you want to get along with them, you're kind to them, you trust each other's intentions and you automatically give each other the benefit of the doubt. This relationship typifies the tenets of the Relationship Protocol. So, if you currently have this type of relationship with someone, you can use this as your frame of reference for a "healthy relationship perspective".

By giving the benefit of the doubt for the entire model, you are bringing that healthy relationship perspective to one where that type of communication doesn't come as naturally. This is the most effective way of implementing the RP and increasing your odds for success. You do this for the following reasons:

- **Key Element #1:** Their commitment is to making an effort to improve the relationship, even during challenging times, and

- **Key Element #2:** Their focus is on the relationship, a "we" focus, and valuing you. You are important to them, and
- **Step #1:** They want to get along, not fight, and be closer to you, and
- **Step #2:** They will be kind, and
- **Step #3:** They will not do anything to intentionally hurt you. You trust their intentions, and
- **Step #4:** They will give you the benefit of the doubt, and you will also give them the benefit of the doubt.

The Relationship Protocol model is based on building trust. If both parties give each other the benefit of the doubt for the entire model—the two Key Elements and the Four Steps—both people are essentially relinquishing their history and looking forward together with a fresh start. In time, this then can become the more natural way of relating to and communicating with each other.

The past can be a major stumbling block, and giving the other person the b of d might be difficult because each of you may have different perspectives about your history. Strong emotions and many negative experiences may also make it difficult to get away from old battles and feelings.

Are you willing or able to move forward in your relationship?

If you continue to hold onto the past and don't make a sincere attempt to change by incrementally building trust while improving communication, you have to think about your desire and capability to build a better relationship going forward.

The RP deliberately brings the relationship to the here and now. If you can, put your history aside as you build a new way to relate to each other. Also, because you are building trust slowly, over time you will begin to see if the other person is making a sincere effort and if their actions follow their words. Ask yourself if you are committed to making this relationship work. If so, can you make a decision to move forward and not stay in the past?

On a professional note...

As a clinician, I make an effort to live by this model as best as possible. When introducing the Relationship Protocol, I give each of my clients the benefit of the doubt that they can follow the model to improve their relationships. As long as they are earnest in their efforts, committed, and able to do the work, they can find success with the model. By giving them the benefit of the doubt unconditionally, my energy and belief in them introduces another layer of hope to their struggling relationship.

I offer the same benefit of the doubt to you. Give yourself a fresh start, if possible, and begin with a renewed energy. Take a risk and try something new for the sake of your future, whatever the outcome.

"We're very different from each other. The RP helps us remember that we're not intentionally being hurtful, so we get past things much quicker by talking to each other and giving the benefit of the doubt."

Chapter Eight

HOW TO TALK TO THE IMPORTANT PEOPLE IN YOUR LIFE

The Relationship Protocol helps you develop a positive perspective about your relationships. It can guide your basic daily communication or give you a better approach when uncomfortable situations or conflicts arise. Think of the Key Elements and the Four Steps before you communicate with the important people in your life.

The main points in this chapter can help to ensure the best potential outcome for any significant conversations you may have.

Learn the Relationship Protocol mantra

Let the following two important sentences be your guide when communicating with those close to you. Think of it as your new mantra:

> "I am committed to improving my relationship (Key Element #1), and I value [insert name, if you want] this person (Key Element #2). I want to get along (Step #1), be kind (Step #2), trust their intentions (Step #3), and give them the benefit of the doubt (Step #4)."

Without the model components added, it reads like this:

> "I am committed to improving my relationship, and I value them [or fill in name]. I want to get along, be kind, trust their intentions, and give them the benefit of the doubt."

Allow this mantra to shift your perspective, be your guide for daily communication, and govern your behavior with those closest to you. Read it or say it a few times right now, just to get started. You can also memorize it to help you stay on track.

The suggestions that follow will give you some communication tools and perhaps some confidence, if you need it, to approach the significant people in your life. Remember, when you have something important to say, it doesn't have to lead to a negative or dramatic outcome.

Significant or sensitive topics

A sensitive topic can be any subject that's difficult for you to talk about (no matter what it is). It's likely that sensitive subjects may be different for each of you. The degree to which a topic is sensitive can vary too.

This is a good reason to think ahead and prepare what you want to say thoughtfully and respectfully. You don't want to appear insensitive.

In general, a sensitive topic is something that either of you considers personal and perhaps private. Sensitive topics could be communication issues, expressing your feelings, talking about sex, sexuality, intimacy, money (finances), something about your relationship, parenting, appearance (yours or theirs), and business concerns.

Start by keeping the RP mantra in mind, because it should be the backdrop for the way you communicate with others.

> "I am committed to improving my relationship, and I value this person. I want to get along with them, be kind, trust their intentions, and give them the benefit of the doubt."

Next, think about the following before initiating an interaction:

- How do you want the other person to feel when you are finished talking?
- What's their takeaway from the conversation? For example, do you want them to know
  - ❏ something has happened (good or bad);
  - ❏ your opinion, which might be different than theirs;
  - ❏ your feelings about a topic;
  - ❏ you care;
  - ❏ you've noticed an effort on their part or perhaps no effort;

☐ you're upset; or

☐ you're grateful.

Words and ways to start those delicate conversations

The following are some helpful guidelines for general communication and also for discussing sensitive and difficult subjects.

Timing is important

Check in with the other person before initiating a conversation, especially when it's about a sensitive subject.

It's essential that they are free to talk and that they have the time, interest, and ability to have a conversation with you. Otherwise, you may be setting yourself up for a negative outcome or, at the very least, to be disappointed. This is for your benefit, too, so be sure to ask the other person if it's a good time to talk.

They also need to be available to participate, so start with one of these:

- "Can we talk for a few minutes, Pam?"
- "Do you have time to talk?"
- "Is this a good time?"

If they say yes, then proceed. If not, ask, "When would be a better time?" It tells the other person that you are respectful of their time. You are essentially saying, "You are important to me, and this topic is important as well."

Checking in beforehand is important because you increase the odds of a better result. Here are some suggestions:

- Avoid talking about important topics when the other person is not ready to talk, such as when they are in a bad mood, exhausted, hungry, watching television or answering e-mails, just walking in the door after a long and difficult day, or ready to fall asleep. If you force a conversation, it becomes a potential recipe for disaster. Waiting will be well worth it.

- Have a conversation when both of you can be fully present, alert, and ready to talk and listen, preferably without distractions.

- The initial interaction can be short.

- Ask the other person if they need time to think about the topic. If it's an important topic, you both may want to have more than one conversation.

Your volume and your attitude

If you are anticipating a confrontation, be aware of your tone and your volume. You may begin speaking with an aggressive or annoyed attitude if you are already upset. As the conversation continues, your voice may also get louder, or it may become much quieter, indicating upset or frustration.

When discussing matters that are significant and potentially controversial or negative, it is even more critical to be self-aware. Be aware of yourself before, during, and after the conversation. Pay close attention to your attitude, tone, and the volume of your voice. If you're annoyed or upset, wait until you're calm, and collect your thoughts before speaking. You can always choose to sleep on it if it's an emotional or complicated subject.

What to say? Think ahead

Try to plan what you will say. If you can, have your thoughts organized before you begin speaking. It's sometimes helpful to list your main thoughts or the bullet points you want to address on paper. Be succinct, if possible, and have the paper handy when you are speaking.

Think it through.

It is not advisable to initiate a conversation about a significant or sensitive topic impulsively or without putting in some thought beforehand. If you don't, the conversation may not turn out as well as you hoped. In terms of structuring what to say, state your intent to have the conversation respectfully, try to be brief, don't overwhelm or overload the other person, and stay on point.

Finding the words to start those delicate conversations

As a reminder, you can always start with, "Let's use the RP." or "Think of the RP while we're talking about this topic." This kicks your thinking caps into gear.

A. **Use any of the Step #1 language (or mantra),** especially if you are concerned about a possible negative reaction. You can also use it to reassure them (and yourself) of your commitment to the relationship. Begin with any of the following:

- "I want to get along with you, Gary, and I really do want us to be close, but I'm concerned about…"
- "I want to be closer. I don't want to fight with you. I was hoping we could talk about…"

166

- "Marina, I want to get along with you, and I genuinely don't want to fight with you. Can we make time to finally deal with…"

In Step #1, you are telling the other person that you're going to be more thoughtful in your relationship. If they are familiar with the model, this language will be a clue that you are bringing up a topic with the RP in mind. This will hopefully encourage them to do so as well. If they don't know the model, the language still works as a conversation starter.

B. **Use "I" statements. Then the focus is on you—how you feel—and not pointing a finger of blame.** If you are discussing something negative or that was perceived as negative by the other person, an "I" statement can help to set the tone and lessen the chance for a defensive response.

Be truthful.

> The simplest way to start is to be open and honest: "I want to talk to you about a sensitive subject. This is difficult for me to talk about."

Remember to focus on the "we" or "us," as in "We are in this together" or "We're a team." This stresses the importance of the relationship perspective.

- "I know *we* both want to get along better, but Jackson, when you didn't do XXX, I was disappointed."
- "I want *us* to be closer, and I know you do, too, but I need to tell you that when you said XXX, it made me feel YYY."
- "I'm upset about what happened, Cary. How can *we* make this better?"

C. **When you're not sure how to begin, need clarification, or are confused about what took place, use a starter such as "Help me understand..."**

- "Dario, can you please help me understand about XXX?"
- "I want to understand, Kate. Help me understand what you're thinking (or help me understand what you're doing) because I'm confused (or I don't get it)."
- "I thought we were getting along better, but now I'm unsure. Help me understand about... What were you thinking when you said that?"

For example:

Instead of saying, "When we came home from Mom's house yesterday, you were so quiet. What's your problem, Douglas?"

Try this: "Help me understand why you got quiet yesterday. It was confusing to me."

D. **Start with the good stuff. Positive statement can help to engage the other person.** If there's been any progress, positive changes, or effort on the other person's part, start with that information. Point out what you've noticed, even if there are only small changes. By mentioning the good stuff, you are showing your appreciation and demonstrating that you're paying attention.

Commonalities and progress are a great way to start. Don't just focus on what's not happening or the differences between you and the other person. For example, if the only positive right now is their willingness to listen to you in that moment, take it as a good thing and appreciate it as a reasonable start.

Suggestion: It's good to pause after making the observation so the other person has a moment to absorb the good stuff before you continue.

- "I appreciate that you spoke to your mother about how she treats me. I know you wouldn't have said anything in the past, and I really liked that you spoke to her on my behalf." Pause, and then continue. "Do you think you could also say something to your brother, because he's been difficult lately, too, and I'm still uncomfortable around him. It would mean a lot to me."

- "I know you were just trying to be helpful when you were giving me directions while I was driving." Pause. "But from now on, I need you to just let me drive."

- "I can tell you're trying Claudia and I really do appreciate it." Pause. "I do want to talk to you about something that's bothering me, and I hope that's OK." Then continue after the other person acknowledges that they are free and/or are interested in talking about it. If not, ask, "When would be a good time?" You can add, "because this is important to me," if necessary.

- "Ryan, I know you've been trying to make me feel more important, and it means a lot to me." Pause, and then continue. "I guess that's why I was confused as to why you didn't tell me that your ex-girlfriend has been texting you for the past month. I'm not mentioning this to start an argument, but we do need to talk about this."

Start with those positives.

It's best to express your appreciation for *any* effort that you notice before introducing a more sensitive subject or any important or controversial topic. The goal is for you to encourage the other person's efforts and not focus solely on your complaints. Everyone likes to be noticed, complimented, or told that they are important and valued. No one wants to feel criticized or judged on a regular basis by someone they care about.

E. **Let them know you trust their intentions and are giving them the benefit of the doubt.**
   - "Peter, I want us to get along, and I know you do too." (This simple sentence is about intentions and b of d.)
   - "I trust you, Larry, and I know you didn't intend to hurt my feelings. I'm giving you the benefit of the doubt because I want us to get past this."

F. **Describe the behavior in a few words and how it makes you feel.** Tell the other person if they are doing something that bothers you (or not doing something, which bothers you), and use a calm, neutral tone. Never denigrate, criticize, or insult the other person, because you are attempting to get this person who is important to you to hear what you are saying and respond well. Just describe the behavior using "I" statements.
   - "Connor, I want to talk to you about XXX. I want to tell you that when you do (or don't do XXX) it bothers me, and it feels like YYY."
   - "I want you to know that when you say XXX (or don't say XXX), it makes me feel (think, reminds me of) YYY."

Examples of introducing sensitive topics

- "Dillon, can we make time later to talk about XXX? Let's both pay attention and not let things escalate."
- "Thanks for helping me with the bills yesterday, Hillary." Pause, wait a moment for the other person to respond or acknowledge your statement. Then continue. "There's a lot more to do, but we made a good dent. I hope you can finish it up this week. I really appreciate your effort."
- "Are you free to talk, Julie?" Wait for answer. "I'm not trying to be hurtful or fight with you, but I'm worried about XXX" or "I'm concerned about XXX. Can we figure this out?"
- "I know we both want to get along better, but something you're doing upsets me, and I don't think you know how much it bothers me."
- "Vicky, is this a good time to talk?" Wait for an answer. "I'm looking forward to the party, thanks so much for inviting me. You know I can be shy, and since I'm not going to know anyone there, I just want to make sure you won't run off and leave me alone for a long time, since they're your friends."

Sensitive Topic Example: Between Coworkers

"I know you've been trying to be helpful (the positives) by answering the phones when I'm on break, and I really appreciate it." Pause. "I wanted to thank you for helping with the phone, but I have to ask you to please not file any papers when you're at my desk, because yesterday all those papers

somehow went in the wrong files. I know you were just trying to be helpful, but it kind of messed me up for the afternoon."

Sensitive Topic Example: Speaking with a Friend

"I like spending time together, and I'm glad we've been hanging out more (the positives). I wanted to tell you, though, that I was really upset at how you spoke to me last night when your boyfriend was around. I felt like you wanted me to look stupid by putting me down in front of Dan. I don't know if you realize you were doing that, but it really hurt my feelings."

Avoiding confrontation, real or perceived

Do you fear confrontation or run away from what could be a potential or perceived conflict?

For many people, anticipating a confrontation or being concerned that a conversation will "go negative" is enough to make them back off, shut down, or approach the other person aggressively. The high discomfort level is often disproportionate to the actual situation. These individuals are driven purely by the fear of not knowing what to do or what to say. It only takes a few bad experiences with confrontation or perceived confrontation to make someone uncomfortable addressing those often difficult and sensitive issues.

Then there are other people who seem to enjoy confrontation. The thought of an argument pumps them up, and they get ready for a dramatic and potentially volatile interaction. This more confrontational type of person is typically comfortable with the drama of the fight. Often these individuals simply don't know how else to communicate. They only know how to be combative.

It's a conversation.

When you want to talk to someone about something that's significant or sensitive, think of the interaction as a conversation or a discussion and not as a confrontation. Try to view it as an opportunity to clarify something. These conversations are often about expressing feelings, understanding confusing issues, addressing points of view, resolving problems, or introducing new topics.

There is no need to run and hide from a confrontation, and you certainly never need to get volatile. If you follow the RP, you can introduce a topic, respond appropriately, and defuse the situation.

Remind yourself, "They are not the enemy. I care about this person."

This may sound unnecessary to mention, but it's critical to keep this perspective in mind when there's conflict between you and the other person. Sometimes when you're upset or angry with someone else, you may not think of them as someone who's important to you. Instead, it's common to view the other person as someone who, in that moment, has made you very angry and who you don't like very much. When this happens, they are thought of as the enemy, someone who can hurt you. It becomes more about winning the battle, instead of simply resolving a disagreement.

Therefore, even when you disagree or have an argument, you are both still on the same side, on the same team, in the same family. This is the essence of Key Element #2. Remind yourself that this conflict doesn't change how much you care about this person. It doesn't take away your hurt or anger; it just puts the conflict in the proper perspective. This positive reminder will help to dictate how you communicate with them during and after the conflict.

"Please let me finish."

If you ask the other person to wait until you're finished speaking before they speak, this allows you to focus on what you are saying and complete your thoughts. It also tells the other person that the topic is important to you; hopefully they will be more inclined to actively and patiently listen.

It's a courtesy that's worth asking for. If they interrupt your train of thought, it may be difficult for you to get your full point across, so ask for that consideration.

- "I'm not sure how to say this, Mike, so please let me finish speaking, and then I'll listen to what you have to say."
- "Please let me explain what I want to say, and then I want to hear what you think."
- "Brendan, I'm uncomfortable talking about this stuff, so I made a couple of notes. I don't want to forget anything. Just let me read my notes because it'll be easier for me, and then it'll be your turn."

Listen and hear, and then listen again

Why should you pay attention and actively listen to someone who is important to you?

It's simple—because they are important to you, and therefore, what they say *should* matter to you. Listening to the other person shows them that you care. You also don't want to be the only person talking in a relationship. If that's the case, there are no back-and-forth conversations. Don't just hear what they are saying; pay attention and concentrate on listening to them.

You need to remind yourself that it's not respectful to ignore, talk over, or half listen to the important people in your life. You want those people to know they matter to you and what they say matters too. Not listening or not making time to listen comes off as uncaring, whether that's accurate or not.

By the way, active listening does not include hearing them and offering a grunt in response, or nodding your head while looking at the computer or a book. This doesn't indicate to anyone that you're actually listening or that you care. Also, when someone is speaking to you about something that is important to them, don't be distracted by other people, the television, e-mails, the phone, or anything else. These behaviors can come across as not only uninterested, but also rude and hurtful. Although you certainly don't need to be over-the-top attentive, at the very least be courteous. If you're making an effort to follow the Relationship Protocol and value the other person, make a decision to be a better, more attentive listener.

Sometimes you may have to redirect the conversation or ask the other person if you can delay it.

- If it's not a good time to talk or listen, let them know politely, by saying something like, "Alex, I know you want to talk about XXX, but right now isn't a good time. I'm (fill in the blank: tired, too busy…), but we can talk about it later."

Suggestion: If you say, "Let's talk later," make an effort to remember to bring up the conversation again, or ask the other person to remind you. If you do forget, bring up the topic whenever you do remember, or it could cause hurt feelings.

- When it's taking the other person too long to get to the point, try saying, "I know this topic is important to you, and I am interested, but I'm not fully following. Can you just give me the details for now?"

- When there are distraction or things that are preoccupying your mind, simply explain, "I want to hear what you're saying, Danielle, but there's too much going on here. Can we table it for another time?"

- When you're anticipating what they are going to say, point it out. "I think we've talked about this before, Brent. Are you talking about the XXX? If you are, I want to hear what you're going to say, but I think I know this story."

Caution: Sometimes when we anticipate what the other person may be saying, we can be impatient and come across as uninterested and rude. If this is your situation, let them know that, for whatever reason, you are having a hard time listening to them in that moment, it is not a good time, or the topic is tough for you. Give them some feedback in a respectful way.

- When a topic requires more patience and cooperation than you can give in that moment, be honest and say, "I really want to get along with you and work on our relationship, but I don't feel comfortable talking about this now." Or "I'm concerned our differing views may lead to a conflict. Can we put it aside for now?"

- Admit your feelings when you're uninterested and think the topic is not worth talking about. "I see that you want to talk about this topic, but honestly, I'm just not interested in talking about it. I'm not saying this to hurt your feelings. I'll talk about something else, just not that topic."

Caution: It's OK to be uninterested or unhappy about a subject that's being brought up, but you don't want to be disrespectful.

Bottom line: If you're committed to improving your relationship (Key Element #1, the backbone of the Relationship Protocol), valuing the other person, turning toward them (Key Element #2), and learning how to communicate, then listening with interest and curiosity is certainly a good start. Yet if you are not fully attending to the conversation and *it's an important topic*, be honest with them, or you won't retain all the information that was shared, and it may come back to bite you later.

Not sure how to respond?

If you've been listening and are unsure how to respond, that's OK. Let the other person know in some way that you've heard them, be reassuring, and acknowledge that you've been listening. It's also OK to tell them that you're not sure how to respond. If you tell them in all sincerity that you have been listening to them and you care about what they are saying, but you do not know what to say or how to be helpful to them, they will hopefully appreciate your honesty.

But they're yelling at me or saying mean things

If someone is yelling at you or saying unkind things, you do not have to engage in one-upmanship to see who can yell the loudest or be the meanest. This will only escalate an already tense situation. Remember, it takes only one person to stop an escalating argument.

Instead of jumping in and making things worse, tell them you want to hear what they have to say, but it's difficult because of the way they are speaking to you. This shows that you care and are interested, but also that you will not be participating in their unhealthy negative communication cycle.

Acknowledge that they are obviously upset, but then let them know that the way they are speaking to you is hurtful or mean. Explain that you'd be happy to speak to them at another time, when they are calmer. This reassures them that they're important to you and what they are feeling or thinking matters to you. Most important, if you don't engage, there will be no battle. This is how you soothe and defuse a potentially volatile situation.

Here are some possible responses:

- "I want to hear your opinion, but you're yelling. It's hard to listen when you're yelling. If we take a break, maybe we can talk about this later."
- "Please don't scream at me. I promise, I'll talk to you when you're calm, but not like this."

- "I'm going to hang up the phone now. I'm not being rude. I just can't continue speaking to you when you're being so hurtful."

A note to Mr. or Ms. Fix-It

What type of communicator are you? Do you always need to solve problems or fix issues? Are you so focused on finding a solution that you're not fully listening to the problem? Does it make you feel good to fix things and be helpful? As human beings, sometimes we want to resolve problems, find a quick fix, or cast blame somewhere else. However, with the Relationship Protocol, **we are focusing only on fixing the communication,** because this will ultimately change the relationship.

If you are a fixer, you may get frustrated with the model because, for now, you are not fixing or solving anything except the communication between the two of you.

Important note: Think about your need to solve or fix a problem. It's your need to find the solution, perhaps because you know it will help the other person and/or you feel better about yourself when you are being helpful to someone else. Yet when you are communicating in a healthy relationship, it is not about what you need, it's about the other person who is speaking to you and you connecting with what they need from you in that moment.

Keep in mind the following:

- Often the other person just wants to be heard and understood. They don't need you to jump in and try to fix anything.

- You may not want to sit on your hands or bite your tongue to begin changing this kind of thinking or behavior, but please make that effort. It can be a turnoff if you continue to focus on the solution, especially if this is the only response you offer time and again.
- Perhaps you could listen and then ask how you could help. Then respond based on their expressed request.
- When the communication is better, you may not have the need to fix things as much, because the relationship may feel more satisfying overall.

"Since we started using the RP, we prompt each other constantly to hit the pause button and slow everything down. It's our way of catching those knee-jerk reactions before they escalate."

Chapter Nine

IMPLEMENTING THE RELATIONSHIP PROTOCOL

Now you know that the RP is universal and applicable to your important relationships.

As you read each of the following stories, which are all based on real relationships or a compilation (names, when used, have been changed), think of your own important relationships and how the example might apply to you.

On the other side of the coin, don't read these stories and look to see how different you are from these people; plug yourself in and look for the similarities in how you think and respond (even if it's a different type of relationship example from your own). A positive, open attitude will be much more helpful to you.

Thar she blows! A cup of coffee and other examples of the RP

The following situations and problems illustrate how the RP can be put into action on a broad scale.

"Look Out...Thar She Blows!"

Many people are uncomfortable talking about topics that have even the slightest flavor of a confrontation. They avoid conflicts at all cost. This example shows how avoiding issues and burying them never leads to a good ending. Notice how both individuals apply the model to a potentially complicated and old pattern of communication.

Kristy: "I have a pretty good relationship with my cousin Megan. We're very close in age, and we always get along until there's a disagreement. Megan tends to be very overreactive and emotional. She gets angry sometimes and has no problem telling me her feelings. I'm just the opposite. I become quiet when confronted, just to avoid a fight. I don't like to talk about my feelings, so I avoid conflicts at all cost. I'm never the one to bring up a problem to her or anyone. I act as if nothing is bothering me, even when it is. Unfortunately, I stuff my feelings down, and when I finally do let them out, I get really angry and irrational. My angry blowups end up causing more problems, because we both get out of control and say a lot of hurtful things that we don't mean to say."

The Aftermath

Kristy acknowledges the difficulties she has in expressing herself, especially regarding conflicts. She knows she pushes things down and then explodes, leaving only damage behind. Kristy does this to avoid dealing with her feelings and what she perceives as confrontation.

Her cousin Megan could be seen as a victim of these explosions because, in her mind, everything seems OK until Kristy explodes. She doesn't know that Kristy has been gradually building a powerful arsenal of complaints and distress.

Insert the Relationship Protocol

Kristy's role in the resolution:

Kristy needs to begin by apologizing for this pattern of exploding (Step #3). Her reactions are about her own responses and issues, and they are not meant to hurt Megan. In her mind, Kristy is simply expressing her anger and frustration about whatever has been upsetting her. However, because there are no excuses for angry blowups, after apologizing she can tell her cousin that she wants to get along and not fight with her (Step #1). She can also say she wants to change (take ownership of her life), because she doesn't want to stuff her feelings down anymore.

Megan's response:

Megan accepts her cousin's apology and gives her the benefit of the doubt (Step #4) that she wants to have a better relationship. She also believes that Kristy wants to change her negative pattern of holding things in and then building to an explosion.

Kristy next addresses her reaction to Megan's behavior:

After Kristy is finished discussing her own behavior, she can bring up Megan's behavior. Kristy points out that when Megan gets overly emotional, it's hard for Kristy to communicate with her and not shut down. She's hoping Megan will use this information to pay more attention to her own coping as well (Step #4, giving her the benefit of the doubt).

Megan's role in the resolution:

Megan is also interested in improving their relationship because she doesn't like the battles between them. Megan apologizes to Kristy (Step #3) for behaving in a way that is upsetting to her, even though it wasn't intentional.

Megan has learned that her emotional overreactions upset Kristy and cause her to shut down. Going forward, Megan's role is to learn how to control her emotions better because they are getting in the way of this and perhaps other important relationships.

Kristy's response:

Kristy appreciates that Megan didn't get defensive when she was honest and told her how Megan's emotional reactions make her feel. This encourages Kristy to be more open in the future in talking with Megan. She also gives her the b of d (Step #4) because she believes Megan genuinely wants a good relationship with her.

Kristy's role in the resolution:

Kristy has a personal responsibility to herself and to the relationship because of her tendency to avoid expressing her feelings. In the future, when there is a perceived or real conflict, Kristy promises to try to address the situation directly. If not, she agrees to consider seeking professional help. In the future, Kristy may ask Megan to help her by gently asking if she is upset.

Megan's response:

Megan gives Kristy the b of d (Step #4) because she's grateful that she's going to be more self-aware and not engage in this intense destructive pattern. This motivates Megan, and she also plans to use the RP as a guide for changing her overly emotional ways of communicating.

In this example, both women demonstrated a strong desire to improve their relationship. They are also willing to be open, not defensive, and make changes within themselves for the sake of their relationship. These cousins are focused on the "us" and not the "I." This is a prime example of how the two Key Elements live in the background of all healthy relationships.

Going forward:

If Kristy

- gives Megan the benefit of the doubt, and
- takes a risk, trusting her intentions, and
- tells her how she feels (instead of repressing her feelings),
- she is fulfilling her RP obligation in the relationship.

If Megan pays attention to her own emotions and responds in a positive manner, Kristy will be more inclined to tell her the next time she is unhappy, thus breaking the pattern.

In close relationships, both people take some risks in order to make positive changes. When each person expresses appreciation for the other person's efforts, this also encourages more positive, constructive interactions in the future. Lastly, when both people take ownership of their role in the negative cycle of communication and give each other the benefit of the doubt, trust builds and hope becomes a positive motivator.

"Who's Getting Married? Not Me."

This example shows what can happen when we assume things and fail to check in with the other person. Limited communication is taking place at a time when information would be helpful to both people.

Matthew and Nicole are getting married. For the past few months, while Nicole is excitedly making all of the arrangements for the wedding, Matthew is waiting to be filled in on the details. Matthew quietly offers a few small suggestions but never asks Nicole a direct question about the plans. And she doesn't think he wants to be involved, because he doesn't usually care about these kinds of things.

Another month passes, and Matthew decides that because Nicole hasn't asked for his opinion or filled him in on the details, she really doesn't care about him or his opinion. He believes she's being controlling, and he's getting more and more annoyed. At the same time, Nicole is stressed about everything that needs to be done for the wedding, and she feels alone and resentful that Matthew doesn't seem to care at all. She wonders how he could be so removed from such an important occasion. They begin arguing more often about what seem like small, unimportant issues, and both have started thinking that maybe they are making a mistake getting married.

Think about what is happening to this relationship and the reasons why. Are they using the RP as their guide?

- Do they each have a relationship focus, or are they focused on what's missing and wrong, having more of an "I/me" focus?

- Are they behaving as if they want to get along, not fight, and be closer?
- Are they are being kind to one another?
- Do they trust each other's intentions?
- Are they giving each other the benefit of the doubt?
- Are they jumping to conclusions and making assumptions and value judgments?

Here are just a few areas where simple communication could have changed the outcome:

- Nicole began the wedding planning by assuming that Matthew did not want to be involved. She based this on the assumption that, historically, he doesn't tend to care about these things, so she didn't ask or include him.
- Matthew was waiting in the wings for Nicole to involve him in some way. He gave a few minor suggestions but never spoke directly about his desire to be informed or about his concerns.

If only they had addressed these areas from the beginning. Nicole could have asked Matthew if he wanted to be included in the planning, and he could have told her that he would like to be informed along the way. Another opportunity for change was when they started having conflicts, particularly over minor subjects. This is always a big clue that someone needs to stop the action and pay attention to what's going on.

Because they did not clarify those issues,

- Nicole is now stressed and feeling alone and resentful that Matthew is uninterested in their wedding, and

- Matthew had decided that Nicole is controlling and doesn't care about him or his opinions.

Now let's simplify it from an RP standpoint:

Matthew and Nicole are both focused on what the other person is not doing and what's missing. They are not valuing the other person or behaving as if they want to get along and not fight. They are not being kind and are not trusting each other's intentions or giving each other the benefit of the doubt. They are plowing ahead blindly on assumptions.

Regardless of how far along the negativity has traveled, this is potentially a simple fix. One of them needs to hit the pause button. They can then take a moment and unwind what is happening between them. Remember, the RP is often about how we've made the other person feel. Do you want them to feel *that way* about you or the situation? If each person can own their part and not get defensive, because the other person is important to them, this process can be quick and painless.

Either of them can start with the big picture:

"We seem to be really struggling lately. I'm not sure why, but you and our wedding are important to me, and I don't want to fight with you (Key Element #2, Step #1)." Then the couple can talk about how they were both misinterpreting the other person's actions or inactions (Step #4). As long as the conversation takes place in an atmosphere of "we are both committed to bettering our relationship, and we genuinely care about each other" (Key Elements #1 and #2), they can untangle this messy situation.

"Would You Like a Cup of Coffee?"

This example illustrates what can happen when there is a misfire between two people. If neither person is paying attention to what is going on in that moment, things can escalate quickly.

Mother-in-law Susan: "I hate your new coffee maker. It's too complicated, and who has time to read instructions to learn how to use this stupid thing."

Daughter-in-law Naomi: "Well, I like it."

Susan: "Did you really need a new one? I like the old one better."

Naomi leaves the kitchen and goes into another room on the other side of the house. Susan faintly hears Naomi saying something to her. She calls back to Naomi, but Naomi doesn't respond. Susan yells louder to her daughter-in-law the second time, "What did you say, Naomi?" hoping she'll hear her.

Naomi returns and says, "Why are you yelling at me? You are really upsetting me and making me very uncomfortable."

Susan is confused, knowing she raised her voice so Naomi could hear her and not with any intention to make her uncomfortable. Naomi tells her mother-in-law that she feels like she's been putting her down all morning, and she is really upset.

Susan immediately realizes that Naomi might have interpreted her comments about hating the new coffee maker as insulting because Naomi bought the coffee maker and she really likes it. Susan had obviously hurt Naomi's feelings, and she did not want the situation to escalate any further, because that was certainly not her intention.

Insert the Relationship Protocol

Susan's role in the resolution:

Susan quickly says, "Wait a minute, Naomi. There's been a misfire here. First of all, I only raised my voice because you didn't hear me the first time I answered you. I wasn't yelling at you. And I think this was all just a misunderstanding (Step #2). I think I might have hurt your feelings earlier when I said that I didn't like the new coffee maker. I'm so sorry if you heard what I was saying as hurtful. I really didn't mean it that way (Step #3). In my mind it had nothing to do with you. The new coffee maker is confusing for me, and I just don't know how to use it. I would never have commented on it if I thought it would hurt your feelings. And I'm also sorry that you thought I was yelling at you."

Naomi's response:

"I did take it personally because you sounded so critical and upset about the new coffee maker, and I really like it. I felt like you were insulting me. I'm glad you apologized. I accept your apology." (Step #4)

Naomi's role in the resolution:

"I'm also sorry I got so upset (Step #3). I know I can be sensitive sometimes."

Susan's response:

"No problem. I feel badly that you heard my comments as insulting because that was never my intention. And if sometime in the future anything happens between us and your feelings are hurt again, please tell me so we can talk about it. I promise to do the same because I really want us to get along." (Steps #1, #2, #3 and #4)

In this example, Susan was able to respond quickly to her daughter-in-law's reaction and apologize for the misunderstanding, even though she knew her comments were unintentional. If Susan had gotten defensive or angry at Naomi's comments about yelling or making her upset, the disagreement would have escalated or, at the very least, not been resolved in a productive manner.

"A Little Progress Goes a Long Way."

This couple has been using the RP for only a few months. They've made significant progress and have moved away from hopelessness and thinking about breaking up as the only option. They're now both working hard at improving their relationship.

Amanda: "*He screamed at me, and I said to him, 'Why are you screaming at me? It's hurtful to me. Please stop raising your voice.' I actually stopped myself from yelling back at him because I remembered that when I yell back, it always escalated, and I didn't want it to get bad again. I did what I'm supposed to do when he gets upset. I didn't engage, and I stayed calm. I honestly don't even know what he was yelling about.*"

Shane, her fiancé: "*When you told me that you might not go to my brother's house for the weekend, I thought you were threatening me and getting confrontational, and I lost it. I don't like threats or ultimatums. And this week, you locked your keys in the car twice. You keep losing your glasses. You can be so spacey, and it gets under my skin. It's annoying.*"

Amanda took some time and thought about their interaction. She knows she can be forgetful at times, but it isn't something that usually affects Shane. She also remembered that when she asked him about the weekend plans to go to his brother's house, he became annoyed and immediately dropped the discussion. This indicated to her that this was a sensitive subject for him, but she didn't address her observation at that time.

Insert the Relationship Protocol

Amanda's role in the resolution:

Amanda realized she should have brought up the topic using the RP. "I want to get along and not fight. Can we please spend a few minutes talking about going to your brother's house this weekend?"

She also apologized (Step #3) to Shane for not being sensitive and for coming across in a threatening way (even though, inside, she wasn't certain his perception was fully accurate). She apologized because, for whatever reason, he heard her response as an ultimatum, and she didn't intend to come across that way. She put the relationship before the topic or content. The fact that he was upset was more important in that moment than defending her words. After this conversation is over, she can revisit the topic of not meaning for her words to sound like an ultimatum, but for now she wants to resolve the issue at hand.

Shane's response:

Shane appreciated and accepted Amanda's apology, and he gave her the benefit of the doubt (Step #4).

Shane's role in the resolution:

Shane was also self-reflective about their interaction. He realized Amanda's "spacey" behavior had been bothering him all week. He'd also had a stressful week and was probably less patient in general, but he hadn't said anything to her. These little annoyances were brewing, and he stuffed them down. He said, "I could have either mentioned the annoyances to her nicely (Step #2) or just let them go and not hold onto them inside. I also need to be more aware of how the stress at work affects me." Shane realized that Amanda was also right about him being unhappy with his brother. "So it is a tough subject for me, but I should never have yelled at her. I plan to pay more attention to stuffing down my stress and my feelings, so I don't get so angry and start yelling."

Shane apologized to Amanda for yelling and hurting her feelings (Step #3). He acknowledged losing his temper because he let things build up. He then told her that he wanted her to come to his brother's house that weekend because he'd really like her to be there with him.

Amanda's response:

She accepted his apology (Step #4). She also agreed to go to his brother's, demonstrating she cares about Shane and is giving him the benefit of the doubt. They both felt closer and more hopeful about their relationship.

In this example, both partners were able to be self-reflective and to better understand their roles in the disagreement. Both were able to apologize, move forward, and begin trusting their partner's intentions as well as give them the benefit of the doubt.

They both recognized how things had improved since using the RP:

- The interaction didn't escalate and follow the old pattern of arguments in the past.
- They recovered more quickly and have the ability to reduce the number of arguments in the future.

- When Amanda chose not to engage in the argument and instead remained calm, by herself she stopped the entire argument from escalating. Shane was very appreciative of her efforts. He plans to work on being more self-reflective and communicative.

"Now Where Did I Put My Words?"

This example demonstrates how to use the Relationship Protocol when communication doesn't come easily or naturally, even in a business setting.

Helen, a successful businesswoman, is accomplished in her profession, but she has difficulty communicating with Louis, her long-term business partner. Louis thinks on his feet, while Helen tends to be quiet and introverted, and requires more time to express herself. She finds Louis intimidating and at times impatient. For this reason, she often avoids meeting with him unless she is fully prepared with notes in hand.

Helen has not had time to prepare for a meeting, so her avoidance is in full swing. She has also been experiencing anxiety lately as she anticipates having a confrontation with him when they do finally meet to discuss important business matters.

Louis has been interpreting Helen's avoidance as a lack of concern. He is feeling extremely impatient and fed up with what he defines as her "unprofessional" behavior.

After some self-reflection, Helen decides she wants to step out of her comfort zone in an effort to communicate better with Louis. The RP model provides her with a framework to help shift her thinking and give her the words she needs.

Insert the Relationship Protocol

Helen's role in the resolution:

Helen reminds herself that Louis is important to her and that she is committed to improving their business relationship for the sake of their history and the success of their business going forward. She shifts her thinking to valuing the relationship (Key Elements #1 and #2).

Helen begins by approaching Louis to set up a time for their meeting. During the meeting, Helen maintains her professionalism, while she apologizes to Louis for not setting up the meeting sooner, because she knows he is upset with her for the delay (Step #3). She also reassures Louis that their business is very important to her. She's on board 100 percent (Key Element #2). Helen tells him that she wants to have a better relationship with him (Step #1), but sometimes the manner in which he speaks to her is not helpful. She tells him that while she knows his intentions are not to be difficult or intimidating, she finds his extreme impatience to be upsetting and unnecessary (Step #2).

Helen also explains to Louis that while he finds it easy to communicate effectively, even during impromptu meetings, she requires some time to prepare. She admits to avoiding scheduling this meeting with him because, until last night, she did not have time to review the material. Helen then confidently takes out her notes to discuss the issues on their agenda.

Louis's response:

Louis is surprised at Helen's comments about his impatient ways. Because he is also committed to their business and wants to have a good relationship with Helen, he appreciates the way she has spoken to him and the feedback she has offered. He apologizes to her for communicating in a way that was hurtful to her, because that was never his intention (Step #3).

He trusts Helen's intentions, and he gives her the benefit of the doubt that she was being honest with him (Steps #3 and #4). He now believes that she does care about their company, and he's grateful that they were able to address those issues.

Louis' role in the resolution:

Louis tells Helen that he will try to be more patient in the future. He also acknowledges that he was annoyed at her because he had interpreted her avoidance as not caring about their business. He reports being happy that his assumption was wrong.

In general, Louis agrees to be more thoughtful in his communication, because their business runs much more smoothly when they are in sync. He realizes the importance of being a more considerate communicator (all of the RP).

Helen's response:

Helen appreciates that Louis was not defensive or confrontational during their meeting. He actively listened to her and seemed open to hearing what she had to say (Step #2). She was relieved and pleased that the conversation went well and that they both want their business relationship to thrive for the sake of their company.

She trusted his intentions and gave him the benefit of the doubt that he was being honest with her as well (Steps #3 and #4).

Helen didn't realize that her avoidant behavior was viewed as unprofessional or uncaring. This was an eye-opener and a good motivator for Helen to be more proactive and confident in her communication. She also reminded herself that Louis was receptive to listening to her. Helen's takeaway is important: Louis was open and kind during their meeting. His positive response can also help Helen overcome her nervousness and build more confidence communicating with him in the future.

"Me too" interactions: "Whose conversation is this anyway?"

We tend to connect with each other by saying things like, "I know what you mean; me too," "I get you," "I feel that way too," or "I had that same experience." It feels good to connect with one another. I call these "me too" interactions.

Most of the time, "me too" interactions are helpful and positive ways of connecting and bonding with each other. Other times, they can be a big turnoff, resulting in conflicts and causing distance between people. When the negative "me too" cycle gets going, one or both people tend to feel unsatisfied, like they're competing with each other, or believe the other person isn't listening. The conversation usually ends quickly, or it becomes one-upmanship, going around and around, ratcheting "me too" up a notch, until one or both of you are hurt— or possibly decimated. Even if one of you is declared the winner because you were faster with the retorts or your recall of the facts, did anyone really win?

Below is a sampling of three common "me too" interactions. After each one, there's a section called "The Aftermath" and then an "Insert the Relationship Protocol" section that demonstrates how to break this pattern.

If any of these styles of interacting occurs frequently and is not addressed, it can result in ongoing issues for any relationship. The three "me too" examples range from typical to challenging to troublesome.

Typical "Me Too" Conversations

This is the most common type of "me too" interaction, and most of the time it's a nonissue. However, on those occasions when one person is looking for something from the other person, it can ignite a conflict.

Elizabeth: "I'm really feeling down. This was a tough week, and I'm having a tough time."

Bob: "Yeah, I feel down too. We both had a tough week. So, what do you want to do tonight?"

Elizabeth walks away annoyed, and conversation ends.

The Aftermath

Bob's innocent "me too" response of "I feel down too" caused a problem for Elizabeth, and she walked away annoyed. Bob was then left alone, feeling confused. He doesn't understand what is bothering Elizabeth. He thought acknowledging that he also had a tough week and then moving on to another subject was the right way to respond. He thought she was being a little oversensitive by walking away.

It is Elizabeth's responsibility to share her frustrations with Bob so he understands what upset her, especially if it's related to something he said or did. It is Bob's responsibility to pay attention to his "me too" answers and be more open to talking with her as best he can.

Insert the Relationship Protocol

If I'm making an effort, valuing you, and focusing on our relationship, and I want to get along better, not fight, be closer (Step #1), and be kind (Step #2), then I need to respectfully and calmly tell you when you give me an answer that doesn't feel satisfying. In this example, Elizabeth wanted to talk about her tough week. After Bob quickly changed the subject to their evening plans, it became Elizabeth's responsibility to tell him she would like to talk more about her tough week, if that's OK with him. Because Bob also wants to get along, he is interested in hearing about her week.

While using the RP, both people need to be good listeners and observers of the other person. In this example, Bob's role is to find out why Elizabeth was upset, because she and their relationship are important to him (Key Element #2). If Elizabeth consistently feels that Bob doesn't listen or care about her feelings, this can be a recipe for disaster. This one interaction can have a huge domino effect if it's not dealt with at some point. Most of the time, it just takes a brief conversation, and it's no big deal.

In general, it is perfectly fine to say, "Yes, I feel that way too" or "Me too, I'm also feeling down." It's a way of empathizing with someone and bonding with them and their feelings. However, don't assume that's all they wanted from you, especially if they suddenly walk away from you.

After you say, "Me too, I also had a tough week," you might want to ask a follow-up question or make a comment about what they just told you. Ask them something about what they said. For example,

- You can offer some support: "I'm sorry it was a difficult week" or "Is there something I can do for you?"
- You can repeat the same words or feelings that they used in their comments to you. "I'm sorry you're feeling down. Why was it a tough week?"
- It's nice to ask, "Do you want to talk about it?" but only if you're willing to take a moment to actively listen.

These questions demonstrate that you care and want to be supportive.

If you notice that the other person is annoyed, unhappy, or becomes quiet with your "me too" response (or what they may perceive as your lack of a response), try to find out what's going on (Step #3). Ask them, "What's going on?" When they tell you what's bothering them, actively listen and don't get defensive. Apologize if you hurt their feelings (Step #3) and be kind (Step #2). Then they can hopefully give you the benefit of the doubt (Step #4). When you are both satisfied with the conversation, you can move on and talk about your tough week, using the same techniques.

"Me too" tip: Most times, conversations that end with a "me too" leave both parties feeling connected and satisfied. Sometimes you may want to check in and ask, "Was there anything else you wanted to tell me about that?" By showing interest and curiosity, you will help avoid the buildup and possible blowup.

Challenging "Me Too" and "You Do It Too" Conversations

The challenging "me too" example is the old "You do it too!" conflict cycle. Regardless of the topic, it's a common knee-jerk response. This answer usually starts the back-and-forth recriminations. Many people don't even realize they're doing this at the time, because it isn't necessarily intended to result in bad feelings, but it can. The usual response is usually something like, "Too bad, you do it too" or not addressing the initial comment at all: "Oh, well, you do something worse, and I have to put up with that." The initial concern that was brought up by one person is essentially ignored, and a deflective comment ignites the back-and-forth. Be aware and pay attention, because this kind of negative "me too" interaction, even when meant in a harmless manner, can quickly and subtly gain momentum, especially when there's a history.

Elizabeth: "The way you speak to me is so loud and forceful. The tone of your voice is always angry and condescending, and I don't like it!"

Bob: "Yes, you've said that before, and it's just how I talk. I am sorry, and guess what. I don't like the way you talk to me either. You're always sarcastic, and I don't like it!"

This back-and-forth is enough to qualify as a challenging "me too" interaction. Let's add another negative layer, which is also common, because in this example, Bob is planning to win this fight, so he adds, *"You're mean to me, and the kids say you're mean to them too. So don't criticize me, because you do the same thing!"*

The Aftermath

This type of "me too" interaction involves a back-and-forth negativity, and it always leads to a bad outcome if it's not addressed in some way. In this example, both individuals feel unsatisfied, and no one gets their needs met.

If your first response to the other person is, "I know what you're saying about me; but you do it too!" or "You think your situation is bad? You should see mine. Walk in *my* shoes."

How would you feel? Think about it: Someone you care about shared something that was bothering them, and in that moment, you essentially ignored it and threw it back at them with your stronger negative comment. The focus is now on you and your discomfort, not on them or their initial comment.

Were you actually listening to the other person's statement, and do you care about what they had to say? Did you help them feel better now that they have shared their feelings with you? A "you do it too" response leads to a dead end; neither person walks away feeling satisfied, and both typically feel upset and distant. It's also generally a knee-jerk answer and usually doesn't demonstrate thoughtfulness or caring about the other person or the relationship in that moment. The conversation becomes a battle about winning the point, making your point, not caring, and/or not listening. One of you is turned away, hurt, or insulted, and essentially fights back to make a point or win.

Insert the Relationship Protocol

Elizabeth's comments to Bob appear honest, and it doesn't seem she is intentionally trying to insult him (Step #3). However, we don't know their history. If this is a longstanding issue and a sensitive one, she might want to think about how best to present her feelings to him.

Because this is a potentially problematic and sensitive topic, a good way for Elizabeth to begin the conversation is to ask Bob, "Is this a good time to talk?" If Elizabeth starts the conversation with the steps by telling him she wants to get along better and addresses her feelings toward Bob in a kind way (Steps #1 and #2), she has a better chance at a positive result. The success comes because she is reminding him before she starts that she is making an effort and that their relationship is important to her. She's not jumping in quickly or carelessly talking about her problems with him. She can always start by suggesting they both think of the Relationship Protocol while talking and then pause if things get heated, because she wants to give him the benefit of the doubt (Step #4). Essentially, she's asking him to listen to her, let her finish whatever she has to say, and think before he responds. She reminds him that she's trying to tell him something that's important to her and not hurt his feelings (Step #3).

In this example, Bob also needs some guidance. He needs to learn to pause and take a moment to think before responding, especially if, as in the past, these kinds of interactions have led to conflicts. In healthy relationships (and when using the RP), we try to listen and respond to what the other person is saying. Bob might start by validating his wife's feelings and apologizing for speaking to her in a way that she doesn't like (Step #3). He may be upset with her, disagree with her assessment of how he speaks to her, and even feel justified, but right now none of that matters. The only thing that Bob addresses now is that she is upset with him. He apologizes because he is not intentionally speaking loudly and forcefully to annoy or bother her (Step #3).

By using the RP, he changes his perspective. He can stop and think, "Who do I want to be in this relationship?" and "Is that how I want Elizabeth to feel?" He reminds himself of the RP and that Elizabeth is important to him. He turns toward her because he wants to get along and not fight (Key Element #2 and Step #1 and #2). He may ask her to tell him if he does it again and to point it out nicely. Bob is showing Elizabeth that he wants to try to be better about communicating.

Elizabeth's role is to give him the benefit of the doubt (Step #4). She can tell him that she appreciates him listening to her and give him the b of d that he heard her concern and will try to be more aware of how he speaks to her in the future. Once they begin using the RP, it's not about winning anymore.

Many times, we are already in the middle of a cycle like this when we realize something has gone awry. At any point, you can stop the action or tell the other person that earlier, when they told you about XXX, you might not have been as sensitive as they needed you to be and apologize. Think about using Step #1 language if you find yourself caught in a downward spiral.

After the subject that Elizabeth brought up is done, Bob can then introduce his concerns, but only if they finished talking about Elizabeth's issues and the conversation ended cleanly and without conflict. He could then say, "Are we finished talking about that topic, because I also want to bring something up to you." Or another time he could say, "I'd like to tell you about something that's been bothering me. Can you talk now?" If she says yes, he can continue, following the steps. "I want to tell you something, and I, too, don't want to argue about it. I'm not trying to give you a hard time. I want to get along better, but when you are sarcastic with me, I don't like it, and it's a turnoff."

He could add, "Earlier, when I told you that you were mean to the kids and me, I said it to hurt you. I was angry because I didn't like what you said to me, and it's not true, and I'm sorry." Or "Yesterday when I told you that you were mean to me and the kids, I wasn't saying it just to hurt your feelings. It is something that's been bothering me, and I hope you can think about it and try to be nicer." He could add, "Maybe you're going through a hard time (or working a lot, not feeling well, or whatever it is). I just want us all to get along better."

If you answer with a "me too" response, that's perfectly OK, as long as it's not done in anger or with an aggressive or defensive posture and not just to win the point. If you realize you're guilty of interacting this way, it only takes one of you to say, "I apologize for my quick response. It wasn't nice. I do care about what you're saying. Tell me about it" or "Can we try this again?" And, if your "me too" answer was more about connecting with the other person, you can still ask if there's anything else they wanted to say about that topic. It can't hurt to be curious and check in.

Important "me too" tip: Before you move on to talk about *your* concerns after speaking about their concerns, try to pause, take a break, or ask a question nicely or neutrally: "Did we finish this topic, because I also wanted to talk about XXX." It's important to have closure or some acknowledgment that the first topic is done before you move onto the next one. If you just barrel through, the other person sometimes feels that you're minimizing or not caring about what was just discussed.

Troublesome "Me Too" and the Absolutes:
"Always. Never. Everything."

This last "me too" example illustrates a relationship that is in trouble. They are in a downward spiral, can't get out of their own way, and are essentially stuck. Sadly, they will keep sinking because this pattern of interacting is all they know how to do. Notice how they both speak in absolutes, using words like "always," "never," and "everything." No one wants to be on the receiving end of absolutes. Absolutes are a big trigger, and it feels like a lose-lose situation.

Elizabeth: "I'm not happy with the way things are. I want to get along better, but you're always so negative, and I'm tired of being angry and unhappy all the time. I try to be positive, but you say I'm always defensive. I'm not defensive; I'm just disgusted at the situation. As soon as you start telling me anything, I think, 'Here we go again!' It's all about you being right and me being wrong. I'm always wrong, and I'm tired of it. It's enough!"

Bob: *"I've changed how I talk to you, but it doesn't matter. You still view everything I do and say negatively. Why should I bother changing if you don't notice and you never change? It always stays the same with you, and I'm fed up too."*

The Aftermath

In this example, Elizabeth and Bob are both frustrated and unhappy. This is a "me too" interaction that has reached a toxic level. They're frozen in a negative cycle that's hurtful and completely unsatisfying for both of them. And the resentment between them is building.

Clearly this couple is stuck. Both expressed hope that they've tried to make things better in their own way, but they feel the other person has ignored their efforts. Because at some point both have tried to make things better, we know that they both want a better relationship. This is the hook to get them to begin using or to continue trying to use the Relationship Protocol.

If these individuals are willing to make an effort using the RP, they have a chance at changing the negative communication between them, no matter how long their communication problems have been going on. Even if only one of them is committed to using the RP, change can occur.

Resentment is powerful.

> Resentment is anger and frustration built up over time, and it's poison to healthy relationships. It negatively affects your perspective of the other person and the relationship. As trust decays, things start to feel hopeless between the two of you. People become invested in believing things can't change, and that is scary to both of them. No one wants to feel hopeless, but the resentment cycle will continue to thrive every day until one or both of you is willing to change this destructive pattern.

Insert the Relationship Protocol

"I am committed to improving my relationship, and I value this person. I want to get along with them, be kind, trust their intentions, and give them the benefit of the doubt."

Bob and Elizabeth commit as a couple to put the relationship first. They must acknowledge to each other that they are hurting one another and themselves as well, and yet they really do want to have a better relationship. It can be humbling for them to admit this hurt, especially when they are extremely upset with each other, but they *must* value the relationship and put the other person first. Using the RP Key Elements and Four Steps as their guide, Elizabeth and Bob must strive to be more thoughtful and respectful when speaking to each other.

By changing their thinking and perspective, and using the steps, hopefully they can begin to speak nicely to each other, listen more attentively, and ultimately respond differently to each other.

Why should they respond differently to each other? Think of the RP.

- If you are important to me, I will pause and try to be more thoughtful.
- If you matter to me and I mess up, I will apologize and validate you because I never want to intentionally hurt you.
- I don't want you to be hurt by anything that I did, because I value you and our relationship, and so I apologize.
- I don't need to be right; I need to show you, through my actions and my words, that *you* are what I value most now.
- I hope you will give me the benefit of the doubt, because I want us to start building trust and feel more hopeful.
- As an individual in this relationship, I now know I am responsible only for myself and who I want to be in this relationship.
- If you are still stuck in our old way of relating to each other, I'm still going to try to relate in a more considerate and respectful way. I can control only myself and be the person that I want to be in this relationship.
- And, most important, I will keep making an effort because you and we are worth it!

"Me too" tip: In most of your important relationships, sometimes you will have to decide whether you're invested in staying upset and angry, finding fault, and so on, or if you're invested in making the relationship work. Will you decide to put effort into your relationship to ensure success and inject some hope, or will you continue the negative communication spiral?

"I'm learning how to approach things differently, and it's made a world of difference in everyone else's reactions to me."

Chapter Ten

THERE'S OPPORTUNITY IN SETBACKS. IT'S TRUE!

There are conflicts and struggles in life and, of course, in relationships too. The primary goal is to understand what causes disagreements and to stop them from building steam so they don't result in larger setbacks. In truth, if they do turn into a battlefield, you can still gain helpful information from them that can benefit you as an individual and in your relationships.

Rarely, if ever, does any relationship have a positive trajectory without slipups and problems, so expect them, and try not to get defeated or stalled by them.

Along the way, as you start using the Relationship Protocol, you will take a few steps forward and one or two steps backward while you learn and grow with the model. A certain amount of reverting back to old behaviors is expected, and sometimes there are more of those rough patches than may feel comfortable for you.

Understandably, setbacks are not easy for anyone to deal with, especially if there is a long history of problems and emotions running high. If you're like most people, you tend to get caught in the thick of it and need to take a moment to collect your thoughts. It's important to think about what has taken place and to try to figure out how to best respond.

When you gain knowledge about yourself and your relationship, you gain some control over the situation. Think of this information gathering as a gift. It can

- give you confidence;
- reduce feelings of discouragement;
- minimize or avoid potential setbacks in the future;
- help you to recover faster; and
- motivate you to be a better communicator.

Every day, we can take time to learn from our failures as well as our successes. This is the key to successfully building healthier relationships.

Good news: "What are we doing right?"

If you have a positive interaction, a few good days, or a good week, take a few moments every day—or as often as you remember to do so—and reflect on the positives. Ask yourself some "why" questions, and if possible, discuss them with the other person. You are gathering information to help you better understand what you are doing right—essentially learning *why* it works when it works.

Here are some possible "why" questions for when things are going right:

- "What changed? What are we doing differently? Why did we have a good interaction or a good few days?"
- "Did I notice that it was going well while it was happening?"
- "What did the other person or I do to help make it better?"
- "Was I making an effort to be kind, give the b of d, and trust intentions? Did I use any of the RP Key Elements or Four Steps? If so, which ones?"
- "Was it just an easy week and not much to do with either of us making an effort?"

It's great when things go well. There's an absence of stress. Enjoy it!

Take a moment to notice and appreciate that it feels good to have a positive interaction, a few good days, or a good week. Now think of this good feeling as your positive baseline feeling.

It's essential to pause and enjoy that good feeling because these simple moments start the building process. If you stop the action to notice and enjoy what it feels like to have good interactions with the important people in you life, you will be motivated to continue putting forth effort. Hopefully being more self-aware resonates with you, encouraging and supporting your desire to stay with it. Change happens with these little steps. You are now more present and more aware of yourself and your relationship, perhaps ready to make more measured decisions.

Making changes.

> The only way change occurs is if you are more thoughtful and more deliberate in your actions and your intentions.

Good news about the bad news

Ready for some more good news? If you have a bad interaction, a difficult few days, or a tough week, follow the same directions as above for a good interaction. Use the "why" questions. It's important to take that moment and personally and objectively be self-reflective. Again, if at all possible, consider discussing the questions with the person with whom you had the bad interaction. You are still merely gathering objective information. Only this time, the information will help you to better understand how, when, and what happens to hamper the relationship from working effectively. Be open-minded if you genuinely want to improve things between you.

If you are having a bad day or a bad interaction, don't get disheartened; instead, empower yourself. Take a moment to zoom out and understand why it was a bad day, week, or interaction. Stay curious and interested about what happened. Don't look to judge or analyze. Focus on understanding and learning why things may have gone badly. Perhaps it will motivate you to be even more conscientious using the RP.

Here are the positive interactions questions again, but with a different twist.

- If there were good interactions previously, "What changed? What are we doing differently? Why did we have a bad interaction or a bad few days?"

- "Did I notice it was going badly while it was happening?"
- "Did I or the other person do something that perhaps made it go badly?"
- "Was I making an effort to be kind, give the b of d, and trust intentions? Did I use any of the RP Key Elements or Four Steps? If so, which ones?"
- "Was it just a difficult week, regardless of either of us making an effort or not?"

While it's not easy to think about negative experiences, don't ignore the obvious, and remember, laziness or being too casual and not paying attention only repeats patterns. You are merely gathering information, not dwelling on the bad stuff. This information can be critical to improving and changing your relationship for the better. So collect your thoughts and try to objectively understand what actually happened.

Keep in mind that this can be a much more difficult process
- if you are only looking to find fault and blame the other person;
- if you tend to feel overly responsible for whatever took place;
- if the relationship has been in a bad place for a long time; or
- if the conflicts happen infrequently or around small issues, but when they do arise, they spin out of control.

Let your observations be neutral knowledge in that it doesn't have to be evaluated as good or bad. It is just practical information to help you to learn about yourself in your relationship. You are zooming out to create some distance from the conflict and for objectivity and information gathering. You want to learn something about yourself, increase your understanding, and perhaps develop some compassion or empathy for the other person in the process. In healthy relationships, there is no investment in finding fault or winning the battle.

Notice what, if anything, either of you could have done differently, either during that interaction or to follow the RP during the course of your day. In time, you may notice patterns that contribute or cause the negative slides. You will hopefully become aware enough to ward off and defuse potential conflicts before they even have a chance to get started.

Become an observer.

The ultimate goal is for you to be in your relationship while also observing yourself and the other person. Then you can be more aware and more thoughtful. This concept should be applied in personal and business relationships. This is self-awareness in a nutshell. (There's more on this topic in chapter 13.)

Many people don't have a therapist, life coach, or religious adviser who might ask them those self-reflective questions on a regular basis. In many ways, this professional check-in serves as a reminder to be more self-aware and to pay attention.

If you don't have an organized way of checking in, consider adding a few minutes to your daily schedule or set aside time a few times a week to be self-reflective and curious about your relationship. Think about both the positive and the negative interactions. This is a win-win because objective information will be helpful in learning about yourself and your relationships.

What causes conflicts and setbacks?

Conflicts and setbacks come in all shapes and sizes.

Let's face it, we all get annoyed at some of the people in our lives—it's a part of life. You have to decide which issues are worth the battle. Petty, trivial disagreements, small as they may seem, can often end up as bigger arguments. How you say something by your body language, your actions, and of course the topic you are discussing can all lead to potential conflicts. Misunderstandings and misfires are also big culprits in the land of conflict and setbacks.

Conflicts will happen, but their impact doesn't have to be predestined just because "it's always been that way." They don't have to cause a major setback or battle every time one occurs. This section addresses some of the ways conflicts and disagreements begin, good ways to handle them, and suggestions for recovering from them.

Do any of these potential conflict starters sound familiar?

- "Wow, you're nasty when you're tired!"
- "Why would you say (or do) that? I can't believe you said (or did) that!"
- "That didn't sound very professional."
- "Are you really going to eat another piece of pie?"
- "Your partner is so difficult."
- "I completely disagree with you."
- "I know what you're thinking when you make that face!"
- "I've told you so many times, and you act like I've never said it before."

The reaction or response of the person receiving one of these comments depends on their relationship with the sender and on their own view of the other person, themselves, and the outside world. Given those factors, any of the statements could be taken lightly, as they were hopefully intended—a mere comment or observation meaning no harm. Conversely, the comment might be interpreted as negative, insulting, or hurtful, which usually results in some form of conflict.

In every interaction, both the sender and the receiver have important roles. Here's a helpful tip: think before you speak, and think before you respond. Whether you're the sender or the receiver of these kinds of comments, think about the following questions:

Sender of the comment: Before bringing up a topic or making a quick comment in passing, can you speak respectfully and with kindness? Can you think of the RP model and your desire to get along?

If you shift your thinking to "I want to get along, and I value them," you will speak from a more connected, kind, and non-accusatory place. You can ask that the other person trust your intentions and give you the benefit of the doubt.

Receiver of the comment: Can you trust the other person's intentions and give them the benefit of the doubt? Can you *not* assume that they are looking to start an argument? Instead, perhaps the other person is simply trying to point something out to you or express himself or herself?

Shift your thinking to "I want to get along" before answering. Your response then comes from trusting their intentions and giving them the b of d. When you respond thoughtfully and with respect, you are more open and able to steer away from potential conflicts and from starting a negative cycle.

As both the sender and the receiver, you can prevent most minor disagreements from gaining any momentum if you think ahead before speaking and responding. Here's the gist of the RP: "If I want to get along with you and I value you, then I should be thoughtful in how I communicate with you, how I think of you, and how I respond to you." Shift your thinking to avoid conflicts and change the outcome.

What happens when you are more open and start communicating differently?

Notice how it feels when you change your perspective, trust the other person's intentions, and give them the benefit of the doubt. This subtle modification in your thinking can affect your feelings and your reactions. Most times, things can feel lighter and even less intense.

Conflicts and recovery

If an argument is escalating, consider respectfully removing yourself from the situation as soon as you feel your emotions rising. Let the other person know that you need a break to collect your thoughts, but that you will be back. This can be done calmly and courteously, whether it's in person or on the telephone. The same advice applies when an argument is over. Take some time apart to calm down and think things through more clearly and rationally.

You may need a few moments or much longer—perhaps even overnight—to collect your thoughts and gain some clarity. It's critical to reinforce that you are not disappearing, but simply hitting the pause button to defuse and, hopefully, to gain some understanding about what's taken place. Time also offers you some emotional and perhaps physical distance from the other person and the problem.

Take a few deep breaths. Remember that all relationships have disagreements and setbacks and that you're learning a new way of communicating. This is a process, and it requires time and practice. It's also not easy changing these old patterns, and even the best relationships enter that unpleasant conflict zone occasionally.

Because there will be disagreements throughout your relationship, learning from each interaction is helpful. Take a look at the "why" questions mentioned earlier. Be self-reflective and nonjudgmental, and avoid casting blame indiscriminately. How you handle the conflict makes all the difference. Think, "Is there something that I/we can/could have done differently?" "Do I feel comfortable about how I behaved during that interaction?" "Do I need to learn how to be less explosive, less defensive, etc.?"

Important note: Take a moment to remind yourself that this person with whom you are so angry or upset is that same person with whom you want to have a better relationship. You still want to be kind, give them the b of d, and not do anything to hurt them intentionally. This can be a powerful realization in that moment, and this is the essence of Key Element #2.

Next, let's go back to Key Element #1. You made a commitment to make an effort, even during challenging times. This is exactly why you are asked to make that commitment up front. Remember that the RP framework can help guide you through tough issues. Don't give up now.

Think about how important this person and this relationship are to you. And then remind yourself about Key Element #2 and shift your thinking from how bad things are to what you want to do differently to make the relationship better. Do you need to work harder at being a better communicator? For example, do you need to speak to them respectfully and tell them that every time they say XXX, it hurts your feelings? Think about how to move ahead together. "What do *we* need to do to make this better? Where do *we* seem to get stuck?"

Let the Four Steps be your guide in how you think about the relationship and in helping you communicate. Regardless of how unhappy or frustrated you are right now, encourage yourself to trust that in time you can learn to develop the skills to defuse conflict earlier and recover faster. Don't get discouraged; remember, a few steps forward and one or two backward. It happens.

A word of caution: If you have a volatile or highly reactive relationship, you have to make a conscious and deliberate decision if *you* want to have a better relationship. Reaching out thoughtfully and respectfully to defuse or resolve a conflict is a great start. *You* must commit to be less reactive and explosive, making a renewed effort while also paying attention to yourself. You can only control your own behavior. The personal decision to change your behavior can be life altering, but only if you take it seriously. You may need to seek outside help.

The Relationship Protocol will help you to increase your communication skills, build your confidence, change your perspective, and improve your relationship. It takes time to make this model your own, so stay with it, and it will lead to some positive results. You may still need to seek an outside resource or turn to an expert for additional help, such as psychotherapy, conflict resolution, financial issues, parenting differences, and so on. Be open to whatever reasonable means it takes to make things the best they can be.

What can you say or do after things go badly?

When you approach the other person after a setback, it helps if you can begin with a humble and respectful apology, simply because they matter to you. Shift your thinking to how much you value them, and let this help you to break the ice (Key Element #2). Make an effort to get along and repair the relationship, because this is more important than your pride or keeping a distance. Don't isolate, shut down, or not speak for days; this is the old, unhealthy way of doing things. You can apologize for the fight, for something hurtful you may have said or done, or just because you wish things did not escalate between you. Think about Step #3—"I will never do anything to intentionally hurt you"—and how important it is for resolving conflict and building trust.

You can also begin the conversation by talking about the overall relationship. Think beforehand, "What is the big picture here? Have there been some changes overall?" Start by calmly mentioning one or more positive observations or feelings about the relationship or about the other person, if you can, because this sets a more constructive, open, and encouraging tone. These kinds of conversation starters can help to stop the original argument from continuing and minimize the other person feeling upset or reacting defensively. Use some of the steps language, and talk about moving forward together. For example:

- "I know we've been getting along better, and this is definitely a step back. I care a lot about you, and I don't want to fight with you, Colleen. I really want us to figure out how to get back on track."
- "Kyle, we are really struggling now, but our relationship matters to me, and I hope you still feel the same."
- "I'm hoping that we can work things out, because you are important to me. I do want to get along and not fight."
- "Let's try to start over, Frank, slow things down, and follow the model."
- "I'm so sorry we are having such a tough time. I don't want to do anything to intentionally hurt you, and I know I said some hurtful things in anger. I apologize, and I am going to make an effort to be more thoughtful. Please give me the benefit of the doubt."
- "Joni, I do care about you, and I don't want to fight. Can we try to give each other the benefit of the doubt and start using the RP? If we can't do it alone, I promise to agree to go for counseling."

Start by metaphorically turning toward the other person, shifting your thinking, and then focus on what's happening between the two of you. They will be much less likely to get angry, and it can lessen the knee-jerk defensiveness too.

If you don't get a great response, take a little time to regroup. Don't lash out, but remain kind and thoughtful. Stay focused on your ongoing commitment to the process of improving your relationship, and don't personalize or blame. You can approach them again and ask them to please try to give you the benefit of the doubt, because it's coming from a good, pure place, not an aggressive or negative desire. Bring some patience along too.

Conflicts and suggestions for recovery

The following examples are only a mere token of the infinite possibilities that can cause or result in conflict in a relationship. After each example, there is a "suggested repair." These are generic recommendations that may be used to recover from all sorts of disagreements and setbacks, using the RP model to guide you. The repairs can be applied to many of the conflicts you may encounter in your personal relationships.

"Kevin, why are we screaming at each other about dry cleaning?"

You're having a benign conversation one minute that quickly turns into a disagreement, and then it keeps escalating. You're not sure why something seemingly small turned into such a big deal and how it happened so fast in an otherwise good relationship.

> **Suggested repair:** If you don't stop these kinds of interactions early, they can move at lightning speed, changing from a small blip on the screen to a major setback. It's important to stop the action ASAP and either address what's happening in that moment using the model or suggest tabling the issue temporarily. For example, "This was a big misunderstanding. Please trust my intentions. I don't want to fight about this, and I know you don't either." Or "Can we please take a moment to figure out where we got derailed? Our relationship is important to both of us; I think we can do this." Or "Let's put this aside for now and revisit it when we are both calmer. I'm so sorry if something I said upset you, because that honestly wasn't my intention. Please give me the benefit of the doubt." Don't forget to talk about how to avoid and defuse these kinds of arguments in the future.

"I didn't do that. You're the one who does mean things like that."

The other person is talking about something that's bothering them, and you jump in with an explosive and defensive "You do that, too, but worse…!" These are typically "me too" patterns that can cause escalating problems. They either build gradually or become out of control at supersonic speed. Both people often become impatient and defensive, which feeds the negative cycle.

Suggested repair: No need to get defensive. Listen carefully and then apologize for setting off a negative cycle by not letting them finish. It's also important to recognize the initial topic they were attempting to discuss. After the other person has voiced their thoughts on the topic, it's time for you to mention your feelings on the subject thoughtfully. Pay attention not to jump in next time. Slow things down and stay in the present. One person speaks at a time and stays on topic.

"He said something snippy to me, and he sounded really angry, so I stopped talking to him, and then he stopped talking to me. We didn't speak for a few days until one of us just started talking about something unrelated."

Shutting down, turning off, and avoiding communication are common responses for some people. Typically, when one individual doesn't speak to the other, it's their way of making a strong statement without words, or they're uncomfortable or unsure of how to talk about the situation. Many relationships use this method for days and weeks at a time. Unfortunately, it's sometimes the only conflict resolution they know how to do well. They think it's OK to shut down communication and later just resume speaking as if things have returned to normal, thus avoiding the issue that started the freeze-out.

Suggested repair: Not speaking to each other and/or holding your unspoken angry position for an extended period of time is never good for close relationships. If you aren't ready to talk about an issue, tell the other person you need time. Offer something so you can help repair what is going on between the two of you. You can use the steps language to get you started, but *get started.* Your relationship is important, and it should be treated as such. Wasting days not speaking to each other and avoiding crucial issues is childish, and it continues the cycle of conflict. It only takes one of you to step out of the freeze-out to begin having healthier interactions.

"I don't agree with you, and I never will."
"Well, I don't agree with you either!"

Verbal disagreements can occur about anything from how to deal with someone or something to the color of paint. These kinds of back-and-forth interactions can range from harmless encounters to serious arguments, depending on the relationship and the topic.

Suggested repair: If you say, "I want to get along with you," then you care about the other person's opinion. This does not mean you have to agree with each other, but you need to listen and, at the very least, acknowledge that the other person may have a valid point, even if you don't agree with it. If you don't respectfully acknowledge

THE RELATIONSHIP PROTOCOL

the other person's perspective, they may get more upset and feel admonished or perhaps disregarded. It's difficult for someone to be open-minded and find a positive resolution when they believe that their feelings or opinions do not matter to you. When this occurs, they may become motivated to stay at odds, wanting to prove their point even more. So instead of focusing on disagreeing, stop the action and listen to the other person's opinion. Try to have some understanding or compassion for their viewpoint. This can immediately reduce the heightened level of conflict and give you both permission to agree to disagree.

"I can't believe what I said hurt your feelings."

You said or did something, expressed your opinion, lashed out, or acted out, and your words or actions upset the other person.

Suggested repair: Even if it was unintentional or innocent, or you feel justified because they are difficult or too sensitive, you still need to accept and own that you upset the other person. Unfortunately for you, how you feel or why you did what you did is irrelevant. It's important that you start with an apology because you hurt or upset someone you care about, and this is not how you want them to feel. This is Step #3 in a nutshell.

"I don't want to talk about it Hannah. Everything's fine."

If you isolate, stop talking, push down your feelings, and choose not to communicate, you are creating distance in your relationship, even if it feels justified to you. When one party shuts down communication, the relationship goes on hiatus.

> **Suggested repair:** It's OK to say, "I'm not ready to talk now" or "I don't feel like talking now, but I will talk about it later or another time soon."

However, when you choose to shut down communication, you have an obligation to respectfully inform the other person (whom you care about), as best you can (even in writing if need be), about what is happening for you. Giving the silent treatment or withdrawing without explanation is often hurtful and confusing to the other person. Try to offer them some understanding of your feelings and/or your reasons. Use the model if finding words is difficult for you, or seek professional help if you are unable to step out of your comfort zone to communicate your feelings.

"Why does my drinking bother you so much? It's not a problem for me. It shouldn't be one for you either."

This is an example of when your ongoing behavior is upsetting to the other person and they've repeatedly complained about this behavior. This could be anything from drinking excessively to spending too much time on a hobby to having angry episodes or being inconsiderate. You don't think it's a big deal or a relationship issue, but the other person does.

> **Suggested repair:** Any problem that gets in the way of your relationship needs to be addressed. You don't need to get defensive, but own it and humbly apologize. In truth, this behavior probably needs to change because you are both important to each other and something you are doing is upsetting them. Another option is to discuss the behavior in a way that helps them to understand it better. Either way, issues that get in the way of having a healthy and positive relationship should not be pushed under the rug, because they will continue to grow and multiply.

"You make me so mad. Just leave me alone."

You feel very annoyed, misunderstood, lonely, or unhappy in your relationship. Because you're unsure how to talk about your feelings, you turn off and don't deal with them constructively. You blame the other person, act on your negative emotions, or express yourself angrily, like you've always done. Your frustration and unhappiness keep growing.

> **Suggested repair:** If you do not address your feelings in a constructive or respectful manner, the other person

can't understand how badly you're feeling. And if they're on the receiving end of your negativity, it is probably off-putting and pushing them away, rather than making them or anyone else want to be close to you. This shows how and why the destructive cycle continues to go around and around. If you want to feel more satisfied in your relationship, you have to communicate what you need and how you are feeling in a respectful and thoughtful way at a time when you are not in conflict. It's not about blaming anyone or being right, but wanting to get along and valuing the relationship. Give the other person the benefit of the doubt that they will try to listen if you make an effort to communicate differently.

You talking about the other person: *"What she doesn't know won't hurt her."*

You're hiding something important because you know the other person would take issue with it, not approve, or end your relationship. This includes anything that is secretive, risky, excessive, or self-destructive, such as cheating, flirting online or in person, an eating disorder, gambling, and outright lying.

Suggested repair: When you choose to lie or be secretive, you're taking a risk at the expense of your relationship. Be self-reflective and recognize that this excessive or self-destructive behavior should be addressed before it progresses any further. Impulsive behavior, perhaps for your ego's sake, is betraying something that should be treated as precious. Why are you risking losing or hurting the other person? How do you justify keeping a secret or behaving in a way that could destroy something that is important to you? Don't defend or rationalize your behavior, but figure out what's missing in your relationship or in yourself, and determine what you need to begin building a healthier relationship. Then, if you can, thoughtfully communicate what you need to the other person. Risky behavior and lies are never OK in close relationships. They destroy all trust and cause a deep crack in the foundation of your relationship. You need to take ownership and try to understand the "whys" of your behavior.

"I pay a bill as soon as it comes in. You wait until the day before it's due. That drives me crazy!"

It's common to be in a relationship with someone who functions differently than you do, as if they are your opposite. For example, your general approach or styles of communicating are different; perhaps one is fast paced, the other slow. Or one of you had a traumatic childhood, and the other grew up in a sheltered and innocent environment. Your personalities as well as your past experiences affect who you are today and how you relate to each other. When things don't flow naturally because you often see things differently, this can be a major breeding ground for conflicts.

Suggested repair: If you know you and the other person have differences in approach, values, and/or communication styles, discuss your differences up front, honestly, and gently. Talk about giving each other the b of d while trusting each other's intentions to help ease those issues before they have a chance to escalate. Going forward, make an effort not to jump to conclusions or speak with disrespect about the other person and their approach. When addressing areas of conflict, slow things down, and communicate respectfully and certainly without criticism or blame.

"I barely have time to breathe. I'm so busy taking care of my mom since she's been sick."

You are in the thick of a significant problem or stressor that is affecting your relationship, such as a health issue, major differences in parenting styles, financial problems, and so on. It is easy to get bogged down and stuck in a negative, draining cycle about the issue. Relationships often take a back seat to problems, and this is when things can begin to fall apart.

Suggested repair: Start by acknowledging that there's a very real problem that's having a negative impact on the relationship. Use the RP model to bring up this sensitive subject in a thoughtful manner. Make an effort to be kind and respectful as you begin to address the issue directly.

Chapter 14 has more information about when problems get in the way.

What if they have flaws?

The people you care about have imperfections, and they make mistakes. For example, you can notice their beautiful, otherwise clear, complexion, or you can zoom in on the small pimple on their face. It's your choice. Sometimes you may need to look at yourself more carefully before looking at others through a magnifying glass. This is the essence of being truthful and real about relationships. Taking time to understand yourself better also reduces the number of conflicts and setbacks in your relationship.

You may want to look at your expectations for yourself, the other person, and your relationship. Are they realistic, or are you expecting more and setting yourself and the other person up for failure? Reassess and figure out a better way to think about your relationship, one that benefits both of you and helps move the relationship along.

The important people in your life will disappoint you, make you mad, push your buttons, and more. They are different from you in many ways. Your role is to decide which things are worth letting go, which are worth getting upset about and then discussing, and if applicable, which are true deal breakers.

How does the RP apply here?

Apply the Key Elements: The other person is someone who matters to you, and you value them. It's the "commitment to the process" that helps keep their flaws (and yours) in the proper perspective. Your focus is on the total relationship, committing to valuing them, and not zooming in on negatives.

Next apply the steps: If you are committed to the relationship and you want to get along, not fight, and be closer to them, then it's your role to keep what you perceive as something negative in check. You want to pay attention to what bothers you, but also address your concerns with respect. You're trusting their intentions and also trusting that they are not doing XXX to be intentionally hurtful. By doing so, you are then giving them the benefit of the doubt. Their role is to hear you out and trust your intentions that you are not bringing up the topic just to be unkind. Then they must also give you the benefit of the doubt.

If together you can both communicate concerns using the Relationship Protocol as a framework for your discussion, it will lead you to feel more satisfied, and your relationship will continue to improve. Think of the RP before you bring up something upsetting. Take a breath, hit the pause button, and think before responding. If you're unsure what to say, you can always ask for a moment or some time to collect your thoughts. Use suggestions from chapter 8.

Catching negative interactions before they spiral

If you are aware of your interactions and notice the signs of a potential conflicts brewing, you can make a huge difference in your relationships. When you're more observant of yourself and your interactions, you can make educated, not reactive, decisions about how to communicate and respond.

Sometimes things happen fast and disagreements occur in what feels like lightning speed, even in healthy relationships. To have the best possible scenario for halting or defusing a possible battle, take some control with the following:

- Make a concerted effort to slow down the discussion. It's OK to stop the action, hit that pause button for a moment, and then begin again at a slower speed.

- Remind each other to think of the RP. This can jolt you both into remembering the importance of the relationship in that moment.

- Use the steps to keep the conversation on a better course, such as, "I know we want to get along and not fight" or "Let's give each other the benefit of the doubt and trust each other's intentions."

- Stay in the present. Do not bring up negative references from the past, because they will derail your current conversation.

- Don't have an important conversation if there is any tension in the air, if emotions are high, or if the timing is off. It will be well worth the delay.

- Pay attention to potentially inflammatory statements, old communication patterns, and negative body language.

- Notice if you are veering off topic into an emotionally charged area or if either of you seems to be getting upset. If you are observant, you can gently and respectfully bring the interaction back to a safer place. For example:
  - ❑ "I know we both want to talk about this Chris, but we may need to table it for now."

❑ "Kelly, It looks like we veered from our original topic, and now we're in dangerous territory. Let's either go back to the first topic or table the conversation for another time. It's not worth the conflict now, because we both want to get along."

❑ "It looks like you're getting upset. Before this escalates any further, let's remember the model and take a break for few minutes from talking about it."

❑ "We'll talk about this, just not now. It seems too difficult now. Let's give each other the benefit of the doubt."

❑ "I'm sorry if I said something that upset you. Please give me the b of d, Jeffrey, and trust my intentions."

When something is bothering you, take a moment to decide if it's a topic you need to discuss. If so, use the Relationship Protocol to guide you through it.

If the other person wants to battle or is being difficult or negative, respectfully choose not to engage. You can change the direction and the energy of that interaction and defuse an escalating conflict from the start. Ask them to trust your intentions and give you the benefit of the doubt that you are genuinely not looking to start a conflict.

Those difficult and overwhelming times

All relationships have rough moments and the potential to fall apart quickly. This is where the commitment in Key Element #1 comes in.

Rally your energy to try something new, to use the RP, and not to give in to your familiar negative patterns. Those old reactive patterns are most likely what got you to this rough moment in the first place. You don't want to be complacent or casual. These difficult interactions can erode the foundation of your relationships and destroy everything in their path.

During those intense moments, you're probably feeling highly emotional, uncomfortable, or overwhelmed. Instinctively, you may want to stay and fight it out or take flight.

You may be concerned that the RP isn't going to help you deal with your conflicts. You might be thinking one of the following:

- Why even try?
- It's frustrating. We just keep going back to our old ways.
- We have no idea how to talk to each other.
- I don't think we can do it.
- I'm sure it works for other relationships, just not ours.
- Relationships shouldn't be this difficult.

If any of the above statements sounds familiar, take comfort in knowing that you aren't alone. Anyone who is in a difficult relationship has these same thoughts and feelings at times while using the RP. They are all reasonable and understandable, especially when you are upset.

Here's the reality: you have to start somewhere to make a positive change. If you consistently take your relationship for granted or keep repeating the same negative patterns, you create a breeding ground for conflicts to escalate. You can stop escalations by understanding more about them, catching them early, and using the model. If appropriate, think about compromising as a temporary solution for an ongoing issue, or to at least give it a rest until you can revisit it.

Summary

Conflicts and setbacks will occur. No relationship is going to be perfect or without negative moments. Learning how to communicate better and addressing issues is critical to maintaining a healthy relationship. The goal is to lessen the conflicts so they don't become runaway trains.

It helps if you know those topics or situations that tend to get sticky so you can pay closer attention. When those situations occur, use the RP to discuss the issues, defuse disagreements, table an issue, or respectfully agree to disagree. Make an effort to shift your thinking, and value the other person and the relationship, even during times of conflicts and setbacks. This perspective will guide you to a more open and positive attitude. When you approach a tough subject with sensitivity, an open mind, and a positive attitude, you are bringing your best to the situation.

STOP. REFLECT. NOW IT'S YOUR TURN

Suggestions for all readers

Like anything new, the RP will require your time and practice.

Before you continue reading about the model, consider taking a break and spending some time implementing and using what you've learned about the Relationship Protocol. Take a few days or weeks to practice and experience the model. Experiment with it.

Consistent practice is the best way to learn something new. So take a moment to test it out; it can help you absorb the material.

- Begin by memorizing the mantra, or write down the model and post it somewhere. Print out the model in chapter 16, and keep it with you as a reminder.
- Should you take a break, whatever experiences you have using the model, either good or bad, chalk it up as a learning experience.

But then you must come back and continue reading.

In the next chapters, you will learn more about the RP, yourself, and your relationships. You will be guided through stressors, common issues, stumbling blocks, and more.

It doesn't matter how far into the old negative patterns you are or how often you find yourself slipping back. When you notice a slip off the RP path, simply tell yourself or say to the other person, "I/we need to stop the action, take a moment to pause, and then start using the Relationship Protocol again." Don't place judgments or blame; just observe and be patient. Then when you're ready, come back and read the rest of the book. Be proud of yourself for making the effort.

"If you say something over and over, and you keep doing it, even superficially, it eventually becomes more of a belief. That's how I made it work for me, for us!"

Chapter Eleven

LET'S FOLLOW UP...NOW WHAT? THE RELATIONSHIP PROTOCOL PHASES OF CHANGE AND YOU

These next few chapters will talk about what happens when you start using the model. Hopefully, you have had the chance to use the RP and have given it a good test drive. Truthfully, no matter what the results, it's a positive direction at this beginning stage, just for making the effort.

Here's why: You've probably changed your thinking, even slightly. If you made an effort to speak differently to someone or to look at or think about a person or situation differently, you're on the right track. This is exactly where you want to be. The changes are not about big gestures, but more about taking a moment to think and respond differently than you have in the past.

Just "fake it 'til you make it"

In the beginning, using the RP might feel awkward, scripted, inauthentic, "not you," or uncomfortable—but stay with it. After a while, it will begin to resonate, and it will become the natural way you think about your relationship. The "feeling different" will subside, and it will feel more normal and comfortable.

Every time you use *any* aspect of the RP, it becomes more a part of your toolbox. The more you use it through the tough spots, the more it begins to make sense and ultimately becomes a regular part of your communication.

In healthy relationships, it is natural to
- speak pleasantly and respectfully to each other;
- let the other person know they are important to you;
- give each other the benefit of the doubt and trust each other's intentions;
- not fight just to be right or to win the point;
- stop escalating arguments because you want to be in control.

And these are the basic ingredients of the Relationship Protocol.

It may sound simple, but it's not always so easy. Things don't usually move along as quickly as you'd like them to. Even though the RP has simple concepts, you're still changing thoughts, reactions, and behaviors that have been around for a long time. The changes won't be automatic. It only happens if there's thoughtful and deliberate practice over and over again.

When will change come? In three phases: Learn. Practice. Integrate

As you use the Relationship Protocol, you can expect to see some gradual growth and changes in your relationship. Change typically occurs in three phases with the RP, similar to other times when you are changing lifelong patterns and habits. See the diagram below for an illustration of the phases.

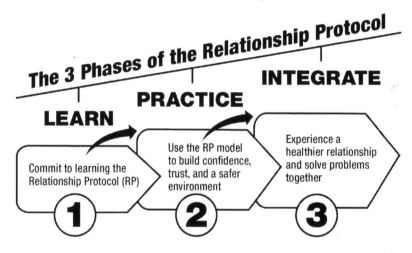

This is a building process that starts at Phase 1. It works only with practice and experience. By learning and practicing the model in Phases 1 and 2, the progression into Phase 3 becomes more organic. Unfortunately, you can't rush through or magically skip over Phases 1 and 2 to get to Phase 3 any faster. You have to put in some time and effort.

Here's why: In Phase 3 you experience a "new normal" as this way of communicating becomes your personal reference for how a healthy relationship is supposed to feel. Communication is more natural and comfortable, not forced or practiced. You're experiencing a more positive way of speaking to each other. When there's an escalating conflict or an unhealthy interaction, you'll spot the difference much quicker. There will also be a marked difference in your communication when there's a slip backward or a setback. And your desire to recover from a setback will also be much stronger and compelling.

The time frame for each phase varies from relationship to relationship. You can't speed the phases along; it's a natural, flowing process. Because change and timelines are interrelated, they will be addressed accordingly below.

Phase 1, Learn: Commit to learning and using the model

In the beginning, there is a narrow focus, because it's only about learning the model.

This is the time to stay in the present and learn how to talk to each other today. Do not attempt to solve big problems, dredge up your history, or deal with issues.

Any serious topics that can lead to conflict are not dealt with for now. Problems and hot-button issues are also put aside. This phase is more superficial because it is only about introducing these new RP communication tools and getting comfortable using them. Addressing problems before you are ready to do so will derail your efforts. You might get discouraged and frustrated before you even have a chance to build healthier and more comfortable communication.

During this phase, make an effort to become more aware of yourself in your relationships. Begin to learn and use the RP communication tools: the two Key Elements and Four Steps.

Within a relatively brief period, a few days to a few weeks, you will hopefully notice some subtle positive changes in yourself and in the other person's reactions to you. Change can occur quickly in this phase, but it begins to root at a minimum within a couple of weeks. During this phase, focus on learning the model only.

Stay with the lighter, simpler topics. Any and all big issues or major complaints get put on the back burner for now. When a challenging issue comes up, acknowledge it and remind each other that *for now* you are putting it aside. You can write it down and revisit the topic in a couple of months. If there is a difficult topic that is unavoidable, use the RP as your script and go slowly as you make an effort to work it through in a more productive manner.

Problems may be connected to how you make the other person feel.

Sometimes a topic resolves itself in time, particularly if it was related to how you were communicating or how you made each other feel. Changing how you communicate will open lines of communication that did not exist before. Longstanding problems can disappear when positive communication occurs. This is the essence of the Relationship Protocol!

Here's an example of a helpful but mild Phase 1 communication: Talking to the other person about how they are grouchy in the morning or how you would like some time to unwind before dinner when you walk in the door after work. In these examples, you can state your observation of their grouchiness or your need for time to unwind in a calm and kind manner. Let them know your intentions are to communicate something you've noticed that bothers you or something you need; your intention is not to be hurtful. You can ask them to give you the benefit of the doubt as well.

At this phase, the entire message is that you want to get along and work on the relationship together; don't bring up anything even slightly controversial or potentially explosive. If you're unsure how to say something, follow the model's guidelines. For example, start by telling them you want to get along and asking them to give you the benefit of the doubt. Because you're still learning the RP, it may feel awkward at first. Just keep referring to the model, take it one step at a time, and if you can, find some humor in whatever happens. There will probably be ups and downs, but just keep moving forward together.

Phase 2, Practice: Use the model until it becomes your new normal

This repetition-practice phase may last a couple of weeks to a few months until you begin to feel comfortable, trusting, and more at ease using the tools. You continue learning by toughing it out, applying the model, reminding yourself to shift your thinking, not getting discouraged, and so on.

During this time of immersion, communication is usually more respectful because it is a more trusting period. Most small conflicts are resolved in a reasonably civilized manner, and when there are conflicts, both individuals are (hopefully) seeking to resolve them in a more productive way. You are making an effort to pay attention to escalations, slowing the communication down, trusting each other's intentions, and giving the benefit of the doubt more naturally. This period is usually lighter, less burdened, and more positive than before. Progress is noticed, but may not be fully trusted yet.

The time frame for this phase is completely individualized, depending on your effort and your relationship. Change here depends on a few variables: the current state of your relationship, your efforts, the health of the relationship and your emotional capabilities, honesty and interest in improving the relationship.

The following relationship factors are significant because they determine how long it can take to make a substantial difference in your life.

- The current state of your relationship: Is this a healthy relationship that needs only some tweaking—for example, do you need to learn how to defuse arguments—or is your relationship on the other end of the spectrum—difficult or damaged with serious concerns about how you relate to each other or mistrust each other?

- The amount of effort you (and, if relevant, the other person) are willing to put into improving your relationship: The effort can be a significant determining factor if you are consistent and committed to the process. You will hopefully begin to notice that in time, and at times, your relationship may have pockets of a lighter and more peaceful feeling. This sign will help you know that things are starting to come together.

- The health of the relationship and the communication: The healthier the relationship, the quicker the process. Conversely, the greater the struggle, the more commitment to the process (Key Elements #1 and # 2) is needed. These kinds of relationships take more self-determination and stick-to-itiveness. They often may require more than a self-help book.
- The emotional capabilities, honesty, and interest of each of the individuals: The disclaimer here is that one or both of you, or the relationship itself, may require more help than simply using this model. Give it a try and see how it goes. If you get nowhere after making a valiant effort for a few months, something else is interfering, either individually or together. Some change should occur with sincere effort. See in chapter 14 to learn more about things that get in the way.

Caution: It is also common for people at this midpoint to feel that they want to give up—but don't!

Instead, make a conscious effort to continue using the model, even if your old patterns of behavior seem difficult or resistant to change. Hang in there! Continue working with the Key Elements and the Four Steps. Learn and follow the mantra.

Examples of Phase 2 communication:
- *"We're certainly not at odds anymore and we can talk about things better than before. We're not as close as I'd hoped we'd be, but it's good enough, at least for now."* There's comfort in the more communicative way of relating to each other. This more relaxed way feels good—better than it has in the past— thanks to the RP.

- *"We still have disagreements, but Margaret and I deal with them a lot better. I used to yell, get really angry, walk away, and not talk to her for a few days. Now I don't yell, walk away, or even ignore her, but I do tell her, 'I'm not ready to have the conversation yet, but I will talk about it with you at some point soon.' Even though the issue isn't resolved, which is annoying for both of us, at least now we're not battling, and we try to remind each other in some way that the relationship is better and important. I do think that, in the near future, I'll be more comfortable sitting down and talking about those topics."* In this example, there is a significant change in the communication before and after using the RP. Disagreements are handled better, keeping the relationship focus in mind, even through those tougher times. Progress has brought some hope and change to a once combative and perhaps stuck relationship.

- *When you're having a conversation, the other person tells you that you are being defensive. Although you may not think you're reacting that way, your first thought is that you don't want them to experience you being defensive. You pause and take a moment to check in with yourself (being self-aware and also trusting their intentions). You then apologize for coming off as defensive, because this made them uncomfortable. After they have accepted your apology and given you the benefit of the doubt, you address your experience with them, if warranted.* For example, upon reflection you may realize that it felt like they were attacking you earlier, so that's why you might have been defensive. You can respectfully tell them that it was most likely unintentional on their part, but at that time, they made you feel uncomfortable. (In this phase you've proven to each other that you both want to get along better, and you've begun to trust each other's intentions and give the b of d.) Hopefully, they apologize for making you feel attacked and uncomfortable, because that was not their intention. You might agree to revisit the original topic another time, knowing that this is now a potentially sensitive subject to discuss.

Will you decide to remain at Phase 2?

Some people in relationships choose to stay at Phase 2. They're grateful to be getting along better, acting civilized, and feeling content that they are more comfortable with each other. If this is your objective, the RP can definitely help you achieve that outcome.

Phase 3, Integrate:
Healthier communication is contagious!

You will know you've arrived at the third phase when you feel comfortable and have confidence and trust in yourself and your relationship. You are more equipped to tackle problems at this phase. The RP is also more integrated into your life. If there are still issues to be addressed, it's now natural to use the RP to speak about them. The model is now more congruent with how you communicate in general with each other. You will still need to remind each other once in a while to trust intentions, give the benefit of the doubt, and not take the relationship too casually.

You must always stay self-aware and focused on the "we." Continue to have respectful and productive conversations.

During this final phase, you now have the skill set not only to trust each other's intentions and to give each other the b of d, but both of you also feel safer and can let yourselves be vulnerable in discussing difficult topics. The environment between you has changed for the better. There's a safety net that envelops your relationship now that did not exist prior to using the RP.

Good news: In Phase 3, because the overall relationship is in a better place, most people find that many of their initial complaints, which were put on the back burner during Phase 1, are sometimes not relevant anymore. Typically, the underlying issues beneath many of those earlier complaints were a lack of communication, not trusting each other's intentions, and/or a lack of a connection. If the relationship has successfully arrived at Phase 3, those complaints are frequently gone or significantly less important to both of you. Also, because the excess stuff (the communication problems, distrust, and emotional reactions) has been removed, there's new clarity about the real issues, if any, that still may exist between you.

This phase tends to bring the real issues or problems to the surface. It also allows educated, well-informed, not impulsive decisions about your relationship to come into play.

If there was a concern about intimacy or finances, for example, now would be the time to discuss it. In general, there is little or no concern about feeling vulnerable or unsafe in the relationship, because trust is a given now. It is a natural part of this connection.

It's also possible that the other person has not been willing or emotionally able to participate fully in using the RP. This becomes telling as you gain more clarity about your relationship's dynamics. During this time, individuals may realize they are not able to stay in a friendship or a marriage because the issues appear to be unresolvable.

> **An example of Phase 3 communication:** a serious talk about intimacy, finances, parenting, differences in priorities, concerns about an addiction, and so on. This phase includes any topic that was previously off the table because someone wasn't comfortable communicating or perhaps because the subject matter was too personal or always led to major battles.

Warning: This is also the phase where you need to pay even greater attention not to take the relationship for granted. Many people slip back into old patterns soon after the "feeling good" period wears off because their relationship is in a better place. As one of my client wisely said, "You can't take a vacation from relationship work. If you do, the old stuff comes creeping back in."

In Phase 3, you certainly don't have to be as vigilant as before, but don't get lazy or casual, or you'll very easily slip back into your old bad habits. Then one or both of you might declare, "This RP doesn't work" or "The results are only temporary." But, quite frankly, these are both false statements. Just print out the RP model or the mantra and remind each other that you want to get back on track. You are not back at square one. It only becomes a major setback if you get complacent, so please pay attention. And at this stage, you should also recover faster from any setbacks, both the little ones and the big ones.

Learn. Practice. Integrate.

This illustration combines the earlier diagram from chapter 1, "How Change Occurs with the Relationship Protocol," and the most recent diagram, "The Three Phases of the Relationship Protocol."

Combining both diagrams shows how and why change occurs during each of the three phases.

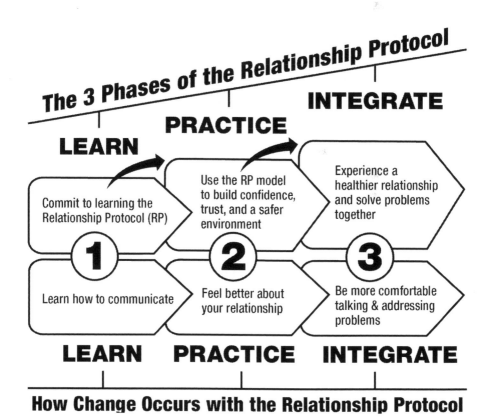

"I learned it's not so easy to change. I did the old 'take it one step at a time and be patient.' It works, so stay with it."

Chapter Twelve

KEEP IT GOING: HOW TO SUSTAIN THE RELATIONSHIP PROTOCOL EVERY DAY

M any relationship conflicts and concerns tend to be similar to others. Think of the topics in this chapter as common themes, problems, or struggles. Every one of these examples has the potential to interfere with and even sabotage your relationship. You may find that your relationship is not completely unique.

As you read, notice the similarities in the emotions and dynamics of these stories to your relationships. Don't focus on the differences. Most of these examples can apply to many different kinds of close relationships.

Change requires some effort

"We forgot."

Sometimes people completely forget to think of or use the RP. If so, they need a pleasant but direct reminder that your relationship will not improve if you don't make the commitment. The only way to change is to be more thoughtful and deliberate in your actions and your intentions. Think about Key Element #1: Commit to the process. This includes making an effort to remember to use the RP and to put positive energy into it, even during challenging times.

This is *your* relationship. Make it important and treat it as a priority, or nothing will change. Put sticky notes in places you will see them that remind you to be the best communicator you can be. This commitment has to come from inside *you*. Copy the RP model, and keep it with you in your wallet or post it somewhere so you can see it more frequently as a reminder.

If you forget to use any of the RP, think about the "whys"—as in, why you aren't putting forth an effort or why you seem to forget? It's important to understand yourself and what gets in the way of working on your relationship. Are both of you willing and able to make the commitment necessary to affect change in your relationship? Do you care enough?

"We were nice for a little while, and then it went back. We quickly reverted to our old negative ways."

This is similar to "we forgot," but here there was a glimmer of hope when "we were nice for a little while." In this case, ask yourself, "What was it like when we were nice to each other? Was it different than usual? Did it feel good? Can we try to behave that way again and try harder to sustain it using the RP model?" Revisit chapter 10 and learn from your setbacks. Remember, most people like when things are going well, even if it's only a small pocket of sunshine in their day. Encourage each other to make the effort to be nice again.

You can also ask yourself those "why" questions that were discussed in the previous example. What changed that you forgot? Do you need to make a stronger effort to remember, or did something happen that set you back into your typical way of relating to each other? This is all very common stuff, so don't get discouraged; use it as information to learn from and move forward.

Share the good stuff

"I noticed a few good changes, but nothing big, so I didn't say anything to Aunt Sandy about it."

We tend to minimize the efforts of others and ourselves, particularly if the changes are not big or grand. In the beginning, forget the grand gestures; take whatever you can get or give for now. Every subtle change, every effort, is important and, if possible, should be noted in some way, especially when you are just learning to use this new communication tool. There are no miracles waiting to happen here, so don't set yourself up. Take a moment to appreciate that you or the other person made a gesture to improve your relationship and build on it.

"Our relationship is a little better now that we're using the RP, but my wife still complains a lot. She doesn't appreciate or notice any of my effort. It's very frustrating."

Sometimes others don't notice the changes you're making, or they don't think they need to comment on small ones. Many times the other people in your life may be too busy or not focused on the relationship to notice or comment. These are common missteps. Stay with it. Here are two suggestions:

1. If possible, speak to your significant other about this issue at a neutral time and in a calm tone. Be respectful and tell them you have been making an effort and you think the relationship is better. Ask them if they notice any improvement and, if not, gently point out your observations. Tell them you're willing to listen to the things that still bother them, but it would be helpful for you if they could also mention any of the positive effort and changes you are making. However, regardless of their initial reaction, stay motivated and keep going, because you're seeing some results and feeling better about yourself.

2. *Always* start with the positives. Remind each other to start with the good stuff. For example, "I hope you know I've been trying lately. I can tell that you are, too, because we seem to be getting along better. I just wanted to check in and see if you noticed that we seem to be making some progress." By starting with the positives and checking in, you will find out their opinion. Also, be prepared if they haven't noticed progress or effort, and don't react negatively. Pay attention and observe yourself while you're speaking to them. Again, make a conscious choice to stay motivated, regardless of whether

or not they noticed progress, because this relationship is important to you and eventually the positive changes will be obvious to both of you.

Avoiding and turtle-like behavior won't help

"My partner tends to isolate. He's uncomfortable talking about feelings and emotions, so he usually avoids talking to me. I get frustrated, and I'm beginning to feel insecure in the relationship and think maybe it's me. How can we possibly use the RP?"

Many times one person is more comfortable than the other talking about their feelings. Reassure them that you are patient and understanding, and you want to get along better. This will hopefully encourage them to begin trusting your intentions and make an effort not to withdraw. These situations can sometimes take time, especially because they usually started a long time ago as a defense mechanism, primarily to avoid conflict. Be patient and look for baby steps at this point. Use the RP to talk to them about how their isolating behavior makes you feel. It sounds like your partner is avoiding what they may perceive as a potential conflict, and you may be personalizing something that has little to do with you and more to do with their insecurities, discomfort communicating, or their desire to avoid fights.

If you try to create a safe and respectful environment, you have a better chance that the other person will gradually come around and begin expressing more. When they do, be very aware to *support their efforts at every step, no matter how small.* If they are unable to come out of their comfort zone, they may want to consider seeking professional help, or you may want to seek help together.

Are you someone who avoids communicating?

If you're an isolator or an avoider, you may be thinking, "If I say something, I'll get in trouble" or "If I show up, I'll have to talk, and then it won't turn out well." Talking to the other person, and communicating in general, may feel like a risk to you. If you can, try to express your concerns about communicating to them. Fill them in so they know what holds you back. They may be interpreting your lack of communication and discomfort as a lack of caring. Make an effort to take even a small step toward communicating your feelings. The Relationship Protocol is designed to help you take that step.

Here are three common examples of avoiding important conversations:

- *"While on vacation with my husband, he seemed annoyed at me for an entire day. I finally asked him what was going on, because I couldn't stand the silence any longer. He said he was annoyed because he had wanted to stay later at the hotel party the night before. I was shocked. He never told me he wanted to stay out later. I would have gladly stayed, if only he had told me."*

- *"I was in a minor car accident on my way home from spring break. As soon as it happened, I thought, 'My parents are going to take my car away. I'm in big trouble.' It wasn't my fault—the guy even admitted he was wrong—but I panicked and decided to stay at my friend's house for the weekend to avoid my parents."*

- *"Sometimes I get nervous because I want to get engaged soon, and I don't know if my boyfriend, Preston, is ready to take that step. I don't want to ask him, because I mentioned it a while back and he got upset. When I think about it, I start to feel anxious, and I kind of freak out inside. He doesn't understand why I sometimes can get impatient, quiet, and unhappy."*

In the examples above, one person didn't express something that was important to them, primarily to avoid a perceived confrontation. None of the individuals felt comfortable or confident in communicating their needs, feelings, or, in the case of the minor car accident, that something that happened. Instead, they each acted out negatively in some way. This is where the change has to start. These individuals have an obligation to themselves and the important people in their lives to become better communicators. If they do this, their needs can be met more fully, and they will have no need to act out and potentially sabotage their relationships.

It can be confusing and difficult to be in a close relationship with someone who holds back their feelings and isolates. Also, if in addition to holding back you then behave negatively in reaction to your undisclosed feelings, it makes it impossible for the important people in your life to feel safe and trust you. They are unsure how to read you or what to expect from you. If this is how you typically behave, take time to learn the RP and use it as a tool for expressing yourself. Ask the important people in your life to participate as well.

You are responsible for yourself

"We were doing OK, and then I said something stupid. I knew I insulted her, but it was already out of my mouth and I couldn't take it back."

Don't fret. It's never too late to apologize for hurting someone's feelings. As soon as you realize you said or did something hurtful, see this as an opportunity. Your opening can come in the next moment, the next day, the next week, or even as it's coming off your tongue. Whenever you can, simply tell the other person you are sorry for having said or done something and you genuinely feel badly about it. You can add the language of Step #1: "I do want to get along with you and not fight. I want us to be closer, and I'm sorry."

As explained in Step #3, take ownership and apologize because something you did or said hurt them. It doesn't necessarily change your opinion about what you were discussing, but they are reacting to something, and you don't want them to feel badly. This is why you apologize. You don't want to do anything that intentionally hurts the other person (Step #3). If they are still upset, make an effort not to get frustrated. Stay the course, be patient, and acknowledge your role in making them unhappy.

But, as stated earlier, don't waste anyone's time if you're just offering an empty apology. If you're apologizing only out of obligation and not with good intentions, don't set the other person up or try to fool them into believing that you care about their feelings.

"My sister says I'm always defensive and angry. Maybe I am, but I'm just defending myself when I feel like I'm being attacked."

Use all of the RP: Shift your thinking about how important your sister is to you. Think about trusting her intentions that she wants to get along with you. She may not realize that she's making you feel badly, as if you're being attacked. Give her the benefit of the doubt that her comments are not intended to hurt your feelings or upset you. Then, as a start, respond less defensively and angrily.

Also, if you pause and shift your thinking before you answer her, in that moment you are reminding yourself to respond differently. Make an effort to continue the conversation calmly. Ask her a question to clarify what she's saying, and buy yourself some time to think it through. You may then choose to tell her respectfully that it feels like she's attacking you. You could say, "Can you please try to speak differently to me? I'm sure you don't mean it, but I feel like I'm being attacked" or "I want to talk to you, but I feel uncomfortable with the way you're talking to me." Using the RP, you're telling her that the way she's speaking to you is hurtful, but you're also giving her the b of d that this is not her intention. It only works if you express yourself in a respectful, thoughtful, and kind way.

If she continues in the same manner, pay attention to yourself during the interaction so as not to react defensively, as you have done in the past. Hit the pause button before responding, and use the steps to guide you through the conversation. Also, you may have a knee-jerk defensive or angry response to your sister. This is your moment to be self-reflective. Think about and try to understand why you might react so strongly to her. For example, the topic may upset you, her tone or attitude may irritate you, or some old feelings from your past may be creeping into this present relationship. If you're typically defensive and angry when speaking to her, it's possible that your sister may be, in effect, reacting to your similar "me too" response. It's difficult to know how or when these ongoing negative cycles began, but they stop when one or both of you own your behavior and apologize where appropriate.

In general, if someone important to you says you're always defensive or angry, don't ignore them or defend yourself. Instead, pay attention to the person's comment because there's a chance it may be true. If you don't open up to the possibility, it will result in more conflict and distance between you and the other person. It's best to be somewhat humble and own up to your part. Tell them you'll try to be less defensive and more aware.

What if you often respond with anger and intensity?

If you tend to overreact or have an exaggerated defensive or angry reaction and you're unsure why, think about how the other person made you feel in that moment. What are the feelings underneath the anger or defensiveness? Your feelings are valid, yet they may not reflect what is actually happening between you and the other person in that moment, especially if you had a quick, negative, and possibly irrational response. Take time to try to understand where those intense feelings may have come from. And think about how your outburst made the other person feel. Is that who you want to be in this relationship, or in your life? Don't just label yourself as an angry person; do something about it. And apologize for your negative behavior. Own it.

"I don't think I'm always right; I'm just not comfortable apologizing. It doesn't come easily for me. Now my friend Taylor is demanding an apology. She says if I don't apologize, I don't really care about her and I'm not trying to make things better."

Owning your words and your actions are part of the RP. Talk with Taylor at a different time from when she's expecting an apology. Bring up the topic thoughtfully, when there's enough time for a conversation. Explain that it doesn't mean you think you're always right, but that apologizing is difficult for you. Explain that, because she matters to you and you want to have a better relationship, going forward you'll make an effort to apologize or discuss it if she's upset about something you did. It would also help if you offered to work on getting more comfortable apologizing or on understanding why it is difficult for you.

If you often seem to be hurting someone's feelings, try being more thoughtful in your interactions with them. You might ask the other person to trust your intentions and give you the benefit of the doubt as a reassurance to them that you do care.

"I hate sarcasm, but my family is really good at it. We go back and forth, taking potshots or jabs at each other all the time. It's about who can be the most cutting. Sometimes it gets pretty ugly."

If you have a positive relationship where the lines of communication are friendly and clear for all family members and there's no hidden or negative undercurrent, then sarcasm can be fine, even funny at times. However, in relationships with conflicts, sarcasm is typically used as a defense mechanism in which someone lashes out under the guise of humor. Some people don't know how to communicate any other way, and the sarcasm cycle goes around and around. Hurt feelings occur, and it can become a game of one-upmanship with each person trying to win the round.

Ask yourself, "Is this how I want to treat someone who is important to me? Is this who I want to be in my relationships?" Think of the basics of the Relationship Protocol. Step #2 can be modified to read, "I will be kind, not mean or sarcastic." This step sets the tone for building trust and creating a safe environment for healthy communication. You don't need to have the last word or be the most cutting person. You can change the cycle of communication in any of your relationships by choosing not to participate in the sarcastic interactions. Eventually, others may follow suit, especially if feelings are getting hurt in the process.

Here's how to respond to sarcasm that doesn't sound funny to you:

The next time someone speaks to you in a sarcastic way, intending to be spiteful, simply say, "Are you upset with me about something? I'd rather you tell me directly instead of being sarcastic."

Do any of the following situations sound familiar?

- *"I overthink things so much that I actually had a fight with my neighbor in my head. I didn't need to have the actual argument with her because I'd been thinking about it so much. I played the whole thing out in my mind. She didn't know what was going on, except that I was acting really mad at her. I do this a lot. I don't realize it, but sometimes I build stuff up in my head about other people, and I then behave accordingly."*

- *"My uncle is lazy. He cuts me off when I'm talking, and he's selfish too. He needs to know how I feel, so I tell him all the time. What's wrong with that? It's the truth."*

- *"My friend takes forever to get to the point of whatever she's saying. I get impatient, and I'm probably rude to her. How can I get her to make it brief and stay on point? It drives me crazy."*

- *"My colleague is uptight and compulsive. We clash a lot. I'm always left feeling like the bad guy because I usually don't agree with him and maybe I don't always say it so nicely. But he kind of gets on my nerves."*

All of the above examples reveal problems with basic communication issues. In each example, one person could make an effort to speak respectfully to the other person using the steps language to explain that they're upset about XXX. They can present it as "What can *we* do to make this better for both of us?" They need to ask the other person to give them the benefit of the doubt that they aren't intending to be hurtful and then communicate in a more effective way. Start by thinking about Key Elements: (1) commit to making an effort and don't give up, and (2) shift your thinking toward valuing the other person—wanting to get along—and then approach them from that perspective.

Hang in there: Dealing with defeat or discouragement

The examples in this section demonstrate some of the most challenging interactions in relationships. Although the examples are different in many ways, the similarities between them are of serious concern.

Important note: *All* relationships are potentially vulnerable and at risk of getting caught in these dangerous and toxic negative cycles. None is immune.

Each of the following three examples below has similar themes; notice that the following dynamics exist in each of them:

- The situation is recurring; this has happened many times before.

- One or both of the individuals do not feel listened to or heard.

- One or both are feeling very frustrated and upset.

- One or both are having a strong reaction because they believe the other person is not hearing them.

- Most important, the communication between them has shut down.

Now for the examples:

- *"When something negative happens between my father and I, he gets very upset with me, and he doesn't want to hear anything I have to say. He shuts me out as if he doesn't believe anything I say. I feel so twisted about it because there's no relief. He's got a big personality, and I get intimidated. I either get really mad back at him, feel kind of scared, or I shut down. Sometimes I do all three of those things."*

- *"My friend and I go in circles when we have a disagreement. I tell her what I'm upset about, and because she thinks I shouldn't feel that way, she acts dismissively toward me and rejects my feelings. This always ticks me off, and we get into it. I see it happening. It's inevitable every time."*

- *Husband: "I'm always hesitant to talk to my wife, because she gets mad when I say the wrong thing, and she's tough. It could be about work, the kids, the house, almost anything. If I don't answer the way she wants me to, it doesn't end well. Then she starts yelling at me, and I get furious."*
  Wife: "I, on the other hand, always have to be careful when I talk to him, because if I say the wrong thing, he jumps on it and then goes off into his own thoughts and tangents. He stops listening to me and goes into his own world, thinking he knows what I'm saying, and I can't recover. He misunderstands me and then insists he gets it. It's a big mess. I get so frustrated, and then I can't stop crying."

In these examples:

- Neither person is feeling heard or satisfied. Before any situation escalates into one of these familiar bad cycles, you need to take a break. Stop the action and hit the pause button. Your goal is to preempt these toxic interactions before they go into high gear. Do this by stopping and taking a moment (or some more time) apart to collect your thoughts and then reconvene using the RP Key Elements and Four Steps. Use Step #1 language to help start the conversation.

- Both individuals felt misunderstood, frustrated, and most of all, helpless. This is an awful way to feel in any important relationship. Be self-reflective to better understand, if possible, the "whys" of what happens between you.

- Each situation has occurred before between these individuals, and both understood that a reoccurrence was possible and likely. This is exactly why both people need to be self-aware and observe what is going on while they're talking to each other; their observations allow them to catch negative cycles and prevent them from gaining steam. They need to move slowly as they attempt to communicate differently with each other.

Think of stopping the action, pausing, and asking the following questions calmly before anything escalates:

❑ "What happened?"

❑ "What do you think I said? Please tell me because I really didn't intend to say anything hurtful. If I did, I'm genuinely sorry."

Review chapter 10 about how to recover from setbacks.

"I don't like it when things are bad between Harry and I because our relationship seems to go backward. I don't know what I'm supposed to do. It feels scary during those moments, and most of the time I just want to run away."

You are seeking flight, a place to escape the overwhelming negative feelings. It's humbling to look inward and ask yourself to recognize what happens to you in those moments. If you want to have a healthy relationship, you need to stop the action, breathe, calm down, and collect your thoughts. Remind yourself of the Key Elements: (1) commit to the process of working on your relationship, and (2) shift your thinking and say to yourself, "This person is important to me, and I don't want to fight like this any longer."

These times can be very unsettling and should be addressed when the intensity subsides and, hopefully, calm prevails. Take a moment to assess if there is a common thread among the times when things are bad. Then use that information to help you better understand the "whys" of the conflicts and to come up with a plan for addressing these issues in the future, using the Relationship Protocol.

"Again, my mother said something about my job, and I got angry. We both started screaming at each other. I don't know what started it or why I got so mad, but it spiraled completely out of control. How does that happen so fast? And is it really possible to change when it occurs so quickly? I guess this was a big setback. We didn't use the RP at all!"

If you miss the signs and realize that you are now engaged in an all-out verbal battle, such as yelling, or that someone has shut down in anger and frustration, please stop the action and take a break. Use the language of the steps to de-escalate. If possible, physically remove yourself from the situation with respect, and take time to collect your thoughts before you talk with the other person to address what happened. You may want to agree to table the conversation until you are further along using the RP.

After a spiraling, heated argument, everything may feel confusing and distressing to you. Let those feelings be a bold reminder about how quickly things can backslide. It helps to remember the two Key Elements—commitment to the process and shifting your thinking to a "we" focus to value the other person and your relationship—even during these difficult times. Make the effort to think about your relationship and your commitment to your mother, rather than thinking solely about your anger and frustration. If your mother is willing to work together, the two of you can each use the RP and become more self-aware, but if she is not, please do it for yourself. One person can make a tremendous impact, especially in these types of volatile relationships. Don't underestimate your own power and ability to bring about change.

We're finally making some headway

"It feels good to see some positive changes. Do I have to say something to Brittany about everything I notice? It seems excessive and unnecessary."

You don't need to discuss every morsel of change within you or others, but don't withhold your observations either. You're encouraged to mention at least some of the positive stuff between you. Encouragement brings positive changes, hope, and reassurance. Everyone likes to hear a compliment, so if you are comfortable doing so, share what you notice, no matter how small. Pointing out something positive encourages more positive efforts from the other person in the future. They may even compliment you back!

We all like to be encouraged and recognized for our efforts. This is a critical part in developing the positive energy cycle in your communication. Positive recognition goes very far, and it helps achieve your goal of a stronger relationship.

Express your appreciation and gratitude for the other person's efforts, and keep using the RP as a template to guide you. The good news is that positive communication has the power to grow quickly, and it can ultimately obliterate the negative energy and move you both forward.

"So, if I notice progress...then what?"

Take a moment to feel proud of yourself for noticing positive changes and for making some progress. Enjoy it whenever it happens. Can you figure out what you're each doing differently and share what you're trying to do differently? Again, be curious and interested. Verbally express your appreciation and gratitude for the effort the other person is making toward improving your relationship.

The good stuff makes the bad stuff less powerful.

> If you continue to acknowledge the good stuff and the progress you've both made on a somewhat regular basis, a setback won't feel as powerful or as long lasting. You also get to use the good stuff as a marker to remind you both that you can make things better with some effort.

"We were doing great for a few months using the RP model. Everything was different, and we were getting along a lot better. I'm not sure what happened, except that it just doesn't feel as good as before. Nathan and I snap at each other, and we're not as kind or patient as we were just two months ago. I seem to be the only one noticing (or caring) that we're heading back down the old path, and I feel helpless."

This situation happens in almost all relationships. It's terrific when you become aware of the change from a few months ago, because the sooner you realize the "slip," the quicker you can act on it. After pointing out your observation to the other person, take it upon yourself to bring the RP back into your relationship.

Don't engage in blame or continue the negative interactions, such as snapping at each other, and be extra-thoughtful when reminding them of the RP tools. (You want to get along and not argue, and so on.) Remember, sometimes you can only change yourself, and working to improve your relationship can pay off in big ways.

You can get back from a slip.

> The most effective way to get back on track is to tell the other person you want to talk to them when they have a few minutes. Bring up how important they are to you (start with the positives) and that you're genuinely concerned about what feels like a slip to you. If they don't notice, ask them to please trust your observation. Ask them, "What can we do to get back on track, because I know we both felt better when things were going well." Don't blame anyone; just talk about moving in a positive direction.

"We have some family events coming up in the next few months. Every time we go to one of those, it's uncomfortable for Jane and me, or it turns out to be a disaster in some way. Many times the day ends with a full-blown fight. We're finally starting to get along better, so I'm thinking that maybe we shouldn't go to any family things for a while. What do you think?"

Knowing that certain situations or people set you off emotionally is very important. This is when self-awareness helps you be more protective of yourself and your relationship. Until you feel more secure in your healthier relationship with the other person, avoiding potentially bad situations sounds like a positive decision.

The conversations on this topic should always start with the positives about how important the relationship is to you, how far you've come together and your desire to keep it that way. Next, work together to figure out how to proceed and how to deal with these outside stressors. Talk about upcoming events, and determine what each of you needs and wants for these events to be OK for both of you. Can you also come up with a plan that satisfies each person's needs?

Preparing ahead of time is very important when there is a history of problems associated with certain people or environments. If this is a tough situation, consider avoiding or limiting alcohol if you do attend the event, because it can amplify your feelings and create more problems for your already tenuous relationship.

In this example, if attending the family event is too difficult, then decide together to skip it for the sake of your relationship. Protecting a vulnerable relationship is a sign of strength, not weakness. If you choose to go, remind each other of the RP before you get there, and agree to stay positive and focused on getting along.

"How do we keep it going when it works? I'm nervous. It all feels so different and new."

When you commit to putting your relationship first, you begin a new direction of noticing small and positive changes in how you think about, communicate with, and respond to each other.

The best way to maintain the positives and calm your nerves is to talk about it with the other person. Mention it as something you want to see continue, but because it's new, you are understandably nervous about it. There's no need to bring up the topic repeatedly, but it helps to reassure each other and talk about how nice it feels to communicate and get along better. Any acknowledgement of positives is worthwhile.

Talking about the good stuff reinforces it and encourages both of you to continue whatever you're doing to make the relationship better. Consider the following:

- Have a brief conversation about the positive changes and how good your relationship feels. This will help inspire both of you to continue.

- Tell the other person what you've noticed and how you appreciate their effort.

- Give them a hug or another small gesture that indicates more positive feelings between you.

- Compliment them about a good change or effort that you've noticed, or mention that it's nice to get along better.

- If you're not comfortable talking about it with them, just be self-reflective and continue to behave in a positive manner.

Most important, make an effort to keep moving in that constructive direction. Being self-aware and making that effort can and will change the trajectory of your relationship.

Important note on managing expectations: After telling the other person how much you appreciate their effort, *do not* expect or assume that they will turn around and tell you the same. If you pay them a compliment, don't do it just so you get one back, because it may not happen. If you get upset or angry at their response (or lack of response), your positive reason for giving them the feedback in the first place gets lost. This is a common situation in which an individual who starts out with good intentions (pointing out positive effort) ends up in a major argument because they did not get the response they expected.

Bottom line: Compliment or make a positive, encouraging comment because it's a giving thing to do—but have *no* expectations. You are pointing out something to someone you care about because you want to encourage it. Don't make *that* the reason things fall apart again.

Take the lead without expectation.

> Don't do or say things with expectations that may or may not come true at this moment. Do or say something because you want things to be better. Take the lead.

Relationship reality check

- If you've begun using the Relationship Protocol and are on a good path, that's great! Remember to stay with it, because it takes time for something new to become a part of your everyday life. You don't have to feel it, just do it.

- Use both good and bad interactions as information, and learn from them, as discussed in chapter 10. Don't be judgmental or blaming. Take a moment to pause, and try to "zoom out," observe, and be self-reflective.

- Make an effort every day to stay focused on who you want to be in your relationship. Remind yourself how important this relationship is to you, and focus on valuing it.

- Try not to get too overconfident when things are going well, because all relationships can move into the negative zone without too much warning.

Things can change fast, so pay attention and stop the action.

> Even healthy relationships can resort back to old patterns very fast.

- Be curious and interested about the other person and your interactions. Don't assume you know everything. Ask questions about their day and their interests, and be sure to actively listen to their answers.

- As soon as one of you notices that you're veering off the healthy path and heading for a setback, point it out. Tell the other person, "We need to get back on track." Don't complain or blame; use this information to help you get back on track. *These kinds of "mini-intervention" interactions prevent slipups from gaining momentum.*

- If you see a conflict coming, head it off by stopping the action early so it doesn't escalate. Ask your partner, "What's going on?" and pause before responding to their statement.

- When the other person is having a difficult time and you're unsure what to say to them to make them feel better, try one of the following empathic statements:

281

❏ "I'm not sure what to say. I feel badly that you're having such a hard time."

❏ "Laura, is there anything I can do for you?"

❏ "Please help me understand what's going on Jared."

These kinds of statements show compassion and let the other person know you care.

• If they ask you to be supportive or to provide something else they need, and you're honestly not sure what they meant by their request, *ask them!* Don't be embarrassed to ask for more information, and don't assume you know what they meant, because if you're wrong, this may lead to an even bigger conflict.

• Change your thinking to "I want the RP to help me improve my relationship" and "I want to be more effective in my relationship" and "My relationship matters to me."

"I'm calmer now, and our house is calmer too. Coming home used to feel like a chore, but now I actually look forward to it."

Chapter Thirteen

WHEN STRESS KNOCKS, HOW WILL YOU GREET IT?

There are many benefits to having healthy relationships and getting along with those who are close to you. Learning how to communicate better can lighten things up, unburden your world, increase your energy, and even decrease your stress.

Stress impacts communication and, in general, how people relate to each other.

There are times when you may be short-fused with those who are close to you; you may be more impatient than usual or feel overwhelmed, or you may be in the middle of an argument and not quite sure how it started. This is a natural part of being human. We all have good and bad moments. Hopefully, during the not-so-good ones, when nothing seems to be going right, you take a moment to reflect on what's happening within you and between you and the other person. This is what self-awareness is all about.

Many people move through their world quickly, with little time to pay attention or no interest in looking at themselves, reflecting on how they're feeling, managing their day, or thinking about their relationships. Other people tend to put everyone else before themselves. They do for others first, such as family, colleagues, or friends. There are also times and stages in our lives when we are unavoidably busy and overwhelmed with little time for reflection. In each situation, there is often little or no awareness of self, due to limited time, no interest, or no inclination to be reflective.

Imagine going through each day wearing thick, blurry eyeglasses. You might bump into things and miss lots of cues. Your vision could improve dramatically if you only had a good eyeglass prescription. Self-awareness can crystalize your vision and become a guide for communication and coping.

If you tend to have limited or no self-awareness, think about the following questions:

- Do you ever think about or try to understand your moods? Do you know why you get sad, anxious, angry, or defensive?
- Are you aware of how you react to people and things in your life and how others react to you?
- What kinds of things make you feel angry, upset, or feel hurt?
- Have you ever connected physical symptoms, such as chronic migraines, knots in your stomach, tightness in your chest, or neck pain, with stress?

- Will you notice when there's a subtle setback in your relationship?
- How will you deal with an escalating argument or be aware enough to defuse it?
- If you don't have any self-awareness or general understanding of what is happening in your life and its impact, how will you handle a setback?

It's helpful if you pay attention and observe yourself in your world. If you don't, how will you notice and address something in your relationships before it grows into a bigger issue? To be an emotionally healthy and thoughtful person, you must become aware of yourself and how you cope in your daily life with the stressors around you. Even if you are in the midst of a stressful situation or phase in your life, take a moment to zoom in and observe yourself and your surroundings. This is how you learn about yourself and the kinds of things that make you happy or upset you, and how others respond to you.

It is a logical sequence of events. Before you can change something in yourself or your relationships, you need to be aware that it's happening. Then when you become aware of something, you can use the model to discuss your observations.

"That's me in the mirror": What is self-awareness?

Because the entire purpose of the RP model is to change *how* you communicate, it is imperative to begin paying attention to yourself. Here's an example of self-awareness: You do something while knowing that you're doing it, and then you behave using this information. Essentially you are observing yourself and paying attention to what is happening around you, along with your thoughts and feelings, either in the moment or sometime afterward. It's similar to making a mental note of something you've observed; but this time, it's within or about you.

Typically, we are more focused on noticing the other people in our lives and what *they* are or are not doing. In these instances, we are less focused on ourselves.

Try to be curious and interested about yourself and others without being judgmental.

Self-awareness asks you to hold a mirror up to yourself and observe what you are and are not doing. Notice how you think, cope, react, and behave in your relationships and what it may mean. To become more reflective and more thoughtful, pay attention to yourself and the other person. Why? Self-reflection increases your emotional intelligence, and that helps you function better in all your relationships and in life.

If you want to make positive changes and become more aware, then sometime during the day consciously and deliberately stop, pause, and observe what's happening in that moment. This is how you can begin to learn about yourself, your relationships, and your world. It's not the other person's responsibility to know if you're tired, not feeling well, or in a bad mood. When you become aware of these stressors as you go through your day, you'll begin to communicate better and become more self-aware and mindful.

A perfect fit: The Relationship Protocol and self-awareness

- I am committed to improving my relationship, and I value you; you are important to me. These Key Elements set the stage for you to reassure the other person that you're focused on your relationship—not living in a fog, but genuinely interested in what's going on between the two of you.

- Next, if you say, "I want to get along with you, not fight and be closer" (Step #1) and "I will not do anything to intentionally hurt you" (Step #3) and "I will give you the benefit of the doubt" (Step #4), you are agreeing to be responsible for yourself and owning your actions. You are also stating your desire and commitment to pay attention to what happens within you as well as between you and the other person (Key Element #1 again).

- In Step #2, "I will be kind, not mean or sarcastic," you agree to be more aware of how you speak to the other person and how you come across when you're talking.

- Should you choose not to be observant or self-aware, you are not taking full ownership of your behavior or your intentions. It then becomes difficult to build trust or for anyone to give you the benefit of the doubt (Step #4).

Going forward, when things begin to improve in your relationship, not paying attention can result in major setbacks and disappointments. Nobody's perfect, and things do slip by all of us, but making an effort to be more aware of yourself requires only a small effort. Even during the busiest times, some self-awareness can go a long way. Improving your relationship and maintaining it over time depends on being mindful of yourself, your environment, and the other person.

By the way, you always have the option not to make an effort, to stay uninformed, and to keep wearing those blurry glasses. If this is the path you choose, you are giving yourself a pass to behave badly, not taking full ownership, and most important, limiting the possibilities for improving your relationships.

Stressors: Internal and external

Internal and external stressors affect how you feel, how you cope, and how you react to people, things, and situations. Internal and external stressors are relevant to how you communicate with others.

Stress is about the person, the situation, your perceptions, and how it all works together. In other words, how you relate to the world around you—your personality, coping mechanisms, and capabilities; your perception of the stressors; and the number of stressors—greatly impacts how you cope and manage stress on a daily basis.

Internal stressors are inside of you. They're a combination of things, including genetics, emotions, coping skills, history, and experiences with others. Internal stressors tend to be less obvious because they exist inside our bodies. Some internal factors include your perceptions, expectations, beliefs, and even your personality. These factors influence how you cope and also how you perceive your world. Think about it: when you're feeling helpless to change a situation, and it seems bigger than you are, you're most likely to get frustrated and overwhelmed, which then leads to feeling stressed.

External stressors exist outside of you, and they include major events as well as things in your daily life, both large and small: your relationships at home and work, with friends and family, and in social settings. Major life events, which include both positive and negative occurrences, are considered stressful, including marriage, the death of someone close, moving, a job change, financial problems, and retirement. Major stressful events include natural disasters, acts of violence, relationship troubles, or other traumatic events that have a direct or indirect impact. And some daily life stressors include disagreements, an inconsolable baby, feeling disorganized, job problems, long days, and many more. All of these situations can and do have an effect in some way.

Everyone experiences internal and external stressors during the course of each day, and some are compounded over time. Some people minimize stress, while others become overwhelmed and immobilized. Coping strategies are based on many factors, including personality, perceptions, history, and experiences. Some stress is good, and at times it helps you to stay aware and be watchful, but adverse stress can affect your well-being.

Most important, and for the purposes of the RP model, stress affects how you relate to yourself and to those around you.

Check in. Then what?

"How am I doing?" Checking in on *you*

The mayor of New York City from 1978 until 1989 was the late Ed Koch. During his speeches, Mayor Koch would frequently ask the people of New York City, "How'm I doing?" He was known for this popular tagline. He used it as a way of checking in with his constituents to see how he was performing as the mayor of their city.

For our purposes, "How am I doing?" is the question I would like you to ask yourself every day to check in. Imagine what your relationships could be like if you became more self-aware and took responsibility for your words and actions.

- The focus of the check-in is primarily on you.
- It takes only a moment to be reflective.
- As a reminder, you can write down "How am I doing?" and post it somewhere.

Think, "How am I doing?" This question could mean many things, but it only works if it resonates with you. It could refer to any of the following:

- "How am I feeling right now?" Take your internal temperature.
- "What's going on in my world?"
- "How are things affecting me today?"
- "Are there stressors that are bothering me?"
- "Am I focusing on the important relationships in my life?"

This "How am I doing?" check-in is about you as an individual. It asks you to look inward and to think about how you're feeling, managing your day, handling the stressors in your life, relating in your relationships, and so on.

Also use some "How am I doing?" check-in time to think about and better understand your relationships, as mentioned in the previous chapter, using the "why" questions. In time, checking in with yourself and being more aware about yourself and your relationships will become more natural and less deliberate.

Think about this: How do you communicate and handle stress when you are

- tired,
- famished,
- physically sick,
- overwhelmed,
- impatient.
- emotionally exhausted, or
- caught off guard?

Most likely, you won't have your proudest moments when you're experiencing one or more of the above factors. Instead, you'll probably resort back to old, familiar behaviors. By checking in with yourself and noticing the stress factors throughout your day, you can be more in control of your responses and reactions.

Deciding how to react when you feel good and when you don't

I'm feeling good: If you check in and realize you're doing well in that moment and your stress level is low, then pause and acknowledge it to yourself.

It's important to stop and notice your good feelings. This is similar to noticing when you have a good interaction and learning from it. It may sound silly, but it's not. This could be your baseline to use in becoming more mindful. Notice what feeling good feels like: how your breathing might be more relaxed, your energy level raised, your mind and body calmer, and your mood lighter.

Going forward, the goal is to observe when there's a change from that good feeling to feeling tense, stressed, irritable, angry, unhappy, frustrated, or tired. Does your body tense up? Do you notice tightness in your chest, or is your stomach in knots? What happens when you're having a tough day or are in a bad mood, or things are not going well? This is self-awareness, being cognizant of yourself and how you feel in your world—"in your shoes" at that moment. Remember, you do this because feeling stressed can affect how you cope and how you behave with others.

I'm feeling badly: If you notice that you're angry, tense, not feeling well, or in a bad mood, take a moment so you can decide how you want to handle it. The key word here is *decide*. When you are self-aware, you are more in control. You can determine how, or if, you want to respond to a negative situation, your negative mood, or a bad feeling. You can respond by trying to change your mood, or gently and respectfully warn others that you need a little space, or simply be aware of yourself in your environment and respond the best you can.

If you are paying attention to yourself and checking in (How am I doing?), you can then make a decision about how you want to handle and respond to adversity or negative feelings. You've now created a choice about how to respond. Most likely, you won't be as reactive or impulsive in your relationships but perhaps more thoughtful and respectful. You might even be apologizing less too. Without that awareness, you are reacting to others and are not in control of your own feelings and behavior.

In the Relationship Protocol model, you're asked to focus on shifting your thinking from "I" to "us"—focusing on the relationship and what's happening between the two of you. If you are not self-aware, you will not be as present in your relationship, and unfortunately, you will not be functioning at your best.

Coping with stress

In this next example, the person moves through the world quickly without stopping to take notice of what is going on.

It happened one day...

I woke up late for work and rushed out of the house.

I got a flat tire on the way to work, and I didn't have a tire iron.

My cell phone had a low battery, and I'd left the car charger at home.

The tow truck guy who finally came and changed the tire was rude, as if I were doing him a favor.

I knew my boss was mad, so once I arrived at work, I avoided him all day.

At the end of the day, I realized I forgot to eat lunch, and I was famished.

I drove home in traffic.

I arrived home and collapsed, exhausted and mad at the world.

My family only got to see an angry person who yelled at everyone, venting my frustration. I could see they weren't happy with me, but that's life. They should just appreciate that I'm doing my best. Some days are bad days. I'm not going to always be a happy person.

Here's the same example as above, only this time, the person is checking in and using self-awareness to deal with stressors.

Throughout the day, I made a point of acknowledging at each situation that this is one crazy day, filled with frustration (such as running late, having a flat tire, forgetting the cell phone charger, dealing with a rude tow truck driver, and avoiding an unhappy boss) and disappointment.

I had to be very aware that I was on edge, understandably, from one negative thing to another.

I tried to do my best to stay calm and not overreact to anything that came in my path.

I just kept taking deep breaths and checking in, reminding myself that it was just one of those stressful days. I took a walk during lunch, just to step outside for a while, and tried to find humor in the ridiculousness of it all.

I was looking forward to getting home and relaxing, because I could feel the tension in my neck and shoulders.

At the end of my workday, I got into my car and sat for a minute before I left my office parking lot.

I thought about what a crappy day it had been and about how glad I was to have it over. I decided to turn on music that I liked, which always makes me feel good.

I decided to call ahead and say I was stuck in traffic and that I'd had a very bad day. I mentioned that I would need a few minutes to relax and decompress before I spent time with my family.

When I got home, I took a shower, put on comfortable clothes, and decided to enjoy the remainder of the evening.

I knew it was my choice how I reacted to the stress. I decided that I wasn't going to let the stressors ruin the rest of my day. It was a conscious decision. I liked feeling more in control. I also wasn't coming in the door angry and expecting everyone to understand and excuse my behavior.

294

In the second example, the person was acknowledging stressors as they were happening. They were aware of what was going on and made choices throughout the day as to how to respond. When you're paying attention, you can make conscious, measured decisions instead of reacting first and then thinking.

Checking in will help you get through those tough moments and long days.

Don't ruin anyone's day, including your own, because you're having a bad day. Hit the pause button and make a conscious choice about how you want to deal with your stress. Think about "starting the day over" and handling things differently. It's never too late to change the energy and start over.

Living with difficult problems

Sometimes stressful things occur in our lives either for extended periods of time or permanently. When something is going on in your world that's upsetting or negatively affecting you on a regular or long-term basis, it will become problematic if you don't note or address it in some way. This includes anything that, for the most part, is ongoing, long term, having a negative impact on you or your relationship, or feels out of your control.

Many people believe that just because you can't change things—a medical condition, a hot temper, a tough boss—you don't have to do anything to help yourself. This means that the situation should be accepted as such and its impact on you and those around you ignored. While you may feel stuck or resigned to "it is what it is," don't underestimate the daily influence the situation may be having on you and others. It's imperative that you still check in with yourself—"How am I doing?"—on a daily or other regular basis. Then you can decide what, if anything, to do about the stress and its effect. Also, although these kinds of background stressors may not be as dramatic as a one-time crisis or something more obviously stressful, chronic problems can gradually peel away at your coping abilities. It's important to be aware that they do cause stress and discomfort over time.

Talk with those closest to you about what's going on. Ask yourself questions, such as "What do I need to do to cope with this situation?" and "How can I best keep this situation in perspective so it doesn't affect my day-to-day and overall functioning?" This kind of self-reflection reminds you that the stressors shouldn't be overlooked or ignored simply because you don't see a solution. Think about how to best cope with or manage the situation, or those feelings may manifest in other ways, such as depression, anxiety, exhaustion, sickness, or a short temper.

Coping: Pulling out the Relationship Protocol when crisis or trauma hits

Trauma and stress come in all forms, and much of it can be out of your control. Psychologically, we are all affected by stressful events that occur. Some major stressors affect us directly, such as health problems, the death of someone close, financial distress, or a struggling relationship. Indirectly you may have witnessed an act of violence or a horrible car accident, or a family member might be ill. Also, the world around us seems to be changing each day. Many people are victims of natural disasters, floods, earthquakes, tornadoes, and hurricanes wreaking havoc in our communities.

There's violence and acts of terrorism in our own backyards, on college campuses, and in elementary schools and places of business—all closer to home than ever before.

We all have an even greater obligation these days to be aware of ourselves in the context of our environment. When stressful things are going on or you experience a disturbing event, you must, at the very least, note in your own mind that it is a difficult or stressful time. It is not healthy (or smart) to deny or ignore what's taking place inside you, between you and others, or around you. Current events may also trigger old experiences or past traumas. If ignored, trauma and stress can manifest in other ways, such as feeling run-down, agitated, anxious, depressed, or getting physically sick. It can affect your overall functioning. It is never recommended to keep moving forward without any thought or acknowledgement of what has taken place.

Close relationships tend to suffer during stressful times. Statistically, divorce is higher in families that have been hit with trauma, such as a serious illness, death, or a significant loss of some kind. During these times, think about using the RP model to guide you when you are gripped by confusion, sadness, or another overwhelming and powerful emotion.

We all experience grief, loss, and stress differently, so it's important to be respectful and protective of each other's needs. Don't assume or judge how the other person is processing or dealing with what has taken place. Instead, offer kindness and respect. Talk about how you can help each other through this dark and difficult time, and pack some patience too. Just as before, even if you can't do anything about the problem or the situation, take a moment to acknowledge what is taking place.

You can also communicate to the important person(s) in your life any or all of the following:

- Acknowledge that this is a tough time for you and/or both of you.
- Express compassion and kindness for others who are hurting.
- Mention that you're having a difficult time coping and/or that they seem to be having a difficult time.
- Tell the other person that you have been upset and stressed and may have a short fuse, may be overreactive, or may feel on edge, but it's not your intention to be hurtful.
- You might ask each other to give the other some slack and the benefit of the doubt because it is a tough time.
- Suggest that you'd like to make an effort to get through this together. Then it will feel like neither of you is alone during this tough time.

Use the language of the RP Steps:

"I want us to get along and not fight Joe. We need to rally together to get through this."

"I care about you, and I know you're going through a difficult time. I'll try to be more sensitive to your situation and give you the benefit of the doubt before I get upset."

"William, this is a tough time for me. If I'm impatient with you, I'm sorry. It's not you. Give me the b of d and trust my intentions, please."

As you go through your day during times of crisis, be self-reflective and aware of how you're feeling.

- Checking in—"How am I doing?"—is important during difficult times.
- It's critical to make even more of an effort to be kind to others and yourself.
- Patience can be difficult if you're stressed or in crisis mode. If you feel impatient, pause before you jump in with a short fuse on something that was said or done. Remind yourself that the other person's intentions were most likely not meant to be hurtful, and they also may be going through a rough time or may not realize they are upsetting you.
- If possible, take better care of yourself during these times.

The Relationship Protocol tools can be helpful during stressful times. *Lean on them.*

In times of trauma, stress, or crisis, use the tools of the RP: Commit to the process of improving your relationship and valuing each other, especially during challenging times. Using the steps language, being kind, trusting intentions, and giving the b of d will help to defuse potential conflicts, keep things calmer, and enable you to both feel more emotionally supported and connected. And don't forget about hitting the pause button before speaking.

In general, there are many effective ways for managing stress. Figure out what works best for you. It may include taking a walk, listening to music, spending time with friends, going to the gym, or getting a massage. Don't forget to eat well, take a soothing bath or shower, and watch a comedy to get some laughs in. Trim your hectic schedule and allow time for relaxation. And don't forget to breathe; take a few slow, deep breaths whenever you need to calm your mind or body down. Always breathe out a little longer than you breathe in, and try to repeat deep breaths two or three times. Most important, do not ignore stress. Acknowledge it to yourself and to those who are close to you. If necessary, take action steps to deal or cope with it.

If you need extra support and guidance in dealing with stress or trauma, don't hesitate to seek professional help. There are many practitioners who focus solely on grief work and others who specialize in trauma and offer therapy such as EMDR (Eye Movement Desensitization and Reprocessing), which can be helpful during difficult times.

"I've learned to apologize, and sometimes I have to remind him that just because we disagreed, it doesn't mean that I don't care about him or his feelings."

Chapter Fourteen

COMMON STUMBLING BLOCKS IN HEALTHY RELATIONSHIPS

O f the hundreds of relationships that have been helped by the RP, every one of them has had setbacks of some sort and they've fallen into old patterns or gotten caught in a downward spiral. No relationship is immune.

All relationships experience obstacles at one time or another. *How* you respond to these difficulties becomes more important than the actual problem itself. A destructive response can be the most damaging to your relationship. *How* you communicate is significantly more important than the topic you are communicating about.

Becoming self-aware and taking responsibility for your actions and your reactions will significantly enhance your life and all your important relationships.

Are your relationships getting healthier?

Pay attention to how you interact and respond to each other during times of conflict, because this can be a good indicator of whether or not you have healthy communication.

Think about the following two important factors:

1. **How far do you allow the disagreement or conflict to go?** Are you paying attention to not mudslinging and being hurtful, but rather attempting to be kind and to defuse and de-escalate conflicts?

2. **How quickly and thoughtfully do you recover from the conflict?** Do conflicts continue for prolonged periods? Do you feel exhausted, as if you've been through a battle? Do you make an effort to use the RP and remind yourself that this is someone you care about even though you are going through a difficult time?

One way to move toward having a healthier relationship is to change how conflicts play out. For example, if you take time to memorize the RP mantra, you have a better shot at remembering it and applying the messages when you are in the heat of a disagreement. Even if you can't remember the entire model, just grab at any statements that might be helpful to you.

In that moment, people usually recite the part(s) of the RP that resonate for them. In the midst of conflict, you might say,

"Let's hit the pause button" or "We need to give each other the benefit of the doubt" or "Please trust my intentions" or "I really do want to get along and not fight." It's a great defusing technique, and it reminds the other person that the direction of the conflict needs to change before it escalates any further.

There is a definite learning curve here:

- It takes time to understand the core messaging and to know when and how to use it.
- The Relationship Protocol changes how you think, changes your perspective, and teaches you new communication tools. This doesn't happen overnight, and it does require some time for absorption.
- Relationships change as we change, grow, and learn. They are also affected by external and internal factors.
- All relationships have their tough moments. Handling obstacles is one part of the learning curve.

Even if you're highly motivated to use this program and make the necessary changes, there will be bumps along the way as you become a better communicator. These bumps are necessary because they show you that you can handle tough times, which will build a more resilient relationship.

Change can be challenging: Potential stumbling blocks

It may be difficult for you or the other person to do the following:

- Ignore problems that keep getting in the way of learning and using the model.

- Change seemingly automatic knee-jerk reactions.
- Control strong feelings or opinions you may have, whether they are accurate or not.
- Immediately stop and relinquish your feelings or reactions and apologize.
- Give the other person the benefit of the doubt in certain circumstances—or at all.
- Commit to moving forward together using this model without addressing the issues or problems in the relationship first.
- Overcome unrealistic expectations of the relationship or each other.
- Believe that anything is going to make a difference for such big problems or longstanding issues.
- Deal with an uninterested partner who may not be as committed to using the RP as you are.
- Follow a program that seems too scripted or simple, or feels awkward.
- Begin facing the many problems in your relationship, because it's overwhelming and it stops you from moving forward.
- Put in the time or effort, because it may not work or move along fast enough.
- Participate fully, because you need to seek outside professional help. For reasons such as
  - ❑ one of you is clearly stuck, unable to shift his or her thinking and begin building trust;

❑ the problems are more complicated than learning new communication tools; or

❑ the issues are unrelated to communication problems and require additional expertise or skills to resolve.

- Be honest if you have been withholding or lying about something, such as your true feelings about the other person, your lack of desire to improve the relationship, financial problems, or self-destructive behaviors, such as gambling, drinking, drugs, or some other inappropriate behavior outside of your relationship.

- Deal with a crisis situation that is overwhelming for you and/or your relationship.

- Let go of your initial interpretation of an event and shift your thinking to be more positive about the relationship and valuing the other person.

More things that can get in the way

There are also serious issues that can come between you and the other person:

- Problems that are bigger than you can handle now, such as severe differences of opinion, limited coping skills, or issues involving trust or finances.

- Recurring problems in your relationship that are difficult to change or that you refuse to change.

- Issues from your past or from a previous and perhaps unresolved relationship that are affecting your current relationship (for example, past trauma, your childhood, an ex-partner).

- Significant individual and relationship problems that require ongoing support and/or professional guidance.
- Cultural issues, parenting styles, or value differences that cause a rift between the two of you.
- An inability to be self-reflective or open to owning your behavior or acknowledging your part in, for example, hurting the other person.

Don't complain or blame, just do it.

As a starting point, take the Relationship Protocol one step at a time and commit to it. This is the best way to face the stumbling blocks that stop you in your tracks. It's not about being perfect or doing it right; it's about making the effort to put one foot in front of the other and taking one step at a time.

When problems get in the way

Be introspective

When a difficult problem comes between you and an important person in your life, it becomes a big issue in the relationship. The relationship will suffer unless the issue is addressed in some way. Sometimes those challenging problems become overwhelming and even immobilizing. They usually disable progress and make both of you feel stuck, helpless, or out of control. Sometimes one person finds another person's behavior unacceptable. It may concern problems with parenting, anger, drugs, or being too judgmental or controlling. Whatever the problems are, you always have an opportunity to try to change the energy between the two of you and make an effort to get unstuck.

Here's how it starts:

Let's apply the RP, because you're committed to the process of improving this relationship. Part of that commitment is a willingness to look at yourself and see how *your* behavior may be contributing to the problem(s). Can you assess the situation and your role without judgment, but instead with curiosity and interest? Are you doing something that is creating a barrier to improving things between you? Rather than complaining, defending, or blaming, look inward and see if you have some culpability. Give the other person the benefit of the doubt and trust their intentions. Perhaps they are not intentionally being hurtful, but maybe they are simply expressing their feelings or disagreeing with you. Stop responding the same way. What can you do differently to change the energy between you and the other person?

The situation will not get resolved in a productive way unless one of you is willing to change how you communicate or even change your viewpoint. You can't control what the other person does, but you can be more self-reflective. You can take the first step toward making a positive difference in your relationship. The other person will usually appreciate any efforts you make toward resolving your differences. The problem might not be going away, but perhaps it can be put aside for now while you work on having a better relationship using the model. Then, in time, you can always revisit the problem.

Compassion for the other person

Zoom out and try to look at the situation or the relationship from a different viewpoint. Can you put yourself in the other person's shoes? Take a moment and imagine what it might be like to be the other person, how they might feel. What might their experience be like? Remember, they are not the enemy, and you still care about them. Shift your thinking. If you allow yourself to be open to what they might be going through, you can gain some compassion for their position. This may allow you to be forgiving and to move more toward the middle or a resolution.

One word: Compromise

Learning how to communicate can sometimes seem secondary to dealing with your problems. During those times, if at all possible, make an effort to compromise. Compromise usually requires some patience and a little consideration for the other side.

Let's apply the model to a stuck, troubled situation. As in the previous section, begin by using your commitment to the process of improving the relationship (even during challenging times) as your primary motivator. Talk to the other person about wanting to get along and not fight, and instead to be kind to one another. Remind each other that neither of you will do anything to be intentionally hurtful, and lastly, give each other the benefit of the doubt. If you're the only person willing to apply the RP, stay with it. Also, try looking at the problem from a practical standpoint and taking the emotions out of it. Having a different perspective can sometimes improve your ability to compromise.

If you need more support or guidance, consider seeking professional help. Don't rule out going to outside experts for therapy, financial planning, mediation, business consultation, or parenting advice. Outside resources are neutral parties. They bring new information and help take the burden off you to come up with a reasonable solution.

Look within; think about making some concessions for the sake of the relationship. Perhaps others, such as an elderly parent, children, or business colleagues, are involved. If you are unable to compromise for yourself or each other, can you do it for the sake of the others who are directly affected by this issue? Can you use the negative effect you are having on others as motivation to change? You may not be successful using the RP if you can't compromise or put major problems and issues aside for now.

Summary

Ultimately, you each have to decide what you're willing to do to resolve issues that are getting in the way of having a healthy relationship. You need to determine if problems are detrimental to the relationship. Can you talk about the issues rationally and objectively, seeking a solution that makes sense for all involved? If you want to get along and you value the relationship, make an effort to use the belief system of the Relationship Protocol to guide you as you explore your options.

"Everything's not perfect, but even when it's not good, we remind each other that we're not out to hurt each other. I try to focus on taking a moment before responding so I don't get defensive or try to prove her wrong. It helps."

Chapter Fifteen

WHAT IF YOU DON'T HAVE POSITIVE RESULTS?

When the Relationship Protocol doesn't seem to work

This is a big concern for most people that are in difficult relationships. After using the RP model for a period of time, if you find that it isn't working, a few things may be happening.

These are some of the most common reasons for poor results:

- You're not following the model as written, or you may be forgetting to use it, too casual and inconsistent, not fully understanding it, or not completely believing in it.

If this is the case, you will not be successful. History has proven that if you put the time in and make a legitimate effort to use the model, some results—even minimal changes—will usually happen. If there are no results, something else might be going on. Most important, you need to invest in and buy into the RP. Make a copy of the model from chapter 16 and keep it with you as a reminder. Get on board, shift your thinking, and don't underestimate yourself. Have confidence!

- You're stalled, waiting for the other person to make the effort, instead of continuing to use the RP yourself, regardless of their involvement.

Don't wait for someone else. Be responsible and take some control in your life. Use the RP even if the other person is not invested. You can gain some clarity, stronger communication skills, and a healthier outlook. And your relationship can still improve and become much healthier, because you will create that experience for yourself using the tools of the RP.

Let the change start with you. Begin by changing your thinking and being the one who initiates positive communication in all your important relationships. Don't be surprised when others begin to notice; hopefully this will motivate them to come on board too.

By the way, the only disadvantage of having one person use the model is that you won't reach the highest level possible because of natural limitations. But, honestly, some progress is better than no progress.

- One of you seems to be demonstrating minimal effort, may be withholding information, or is not being fully honest about their desire to improve your relationship.

If one of you is not interested in improving the relationship and keeps offering empty apologies, then you or they are not invested in the process or the relationship. Although there may still be some improvement, it will reach only a certain point in your growth together, and progress will be limited and perhaps temporary.

- Sometimes people don't realize that they are invested in staying in the negative cycle of anger or avoidance. They say they are making an effort, but they are unable to participate fully in implementing the model. They aren't ready or able to relinquish their anger or negativity.
- Sometimes one person may be resistant to moving forward. They may be unaware of their hesitation, or they may be well aware of their feelings. Either way, this becomes a huge roadblock, which inhibits progress.

- Sometimes individuals don't trust their significant other enough to give them the benefit of the doubt. Even though the b of d is for each separate interaction, they can't move past old issues and take it one step at a time. They're stuck in the past, perhaps for good reasons, and can't look toward the future and offer the other person the b of d.

These are all examples of when being more self-reflective can help you understand what is holding you back. Ask yourself, "Are we stuck because I can't get past something?" "Is my anger too powerful?" "Am I hesitant to move forward?" Can you make the effort to overcome your hesitations or resistance for the sake of the relationship and because this person is important to you?

Think about seeing the situation or problem from the other person's point of view. Can you understand even a part of how they might be feeling and perhaps have some compassion for them? If so, it may shed some light and break through that stuck feeling. Lastly, can you slow things down and use the model one step at a time?

Do any of the following reasons apply to you?
- The problems you're facing in the relationship are too deeply rooted, and after some significant effort using the model, nothing has changed.
- One of you has a painful history of abuse, trauma, or other disturbing relationship experiences that left emotional scars, making it tough to get close to someone.

- One of you has mental health issues or self-destructive or addictive behaviors that affect your ability to be in a healthy relationship and follow this program.

If any of the above issues are relevant to your relationship, this may be a sign to seek professional help. You may be easily triggered (become irrationally upset) by small things or find it difficult to trust someone who you know is trustworthy. This indicates that you probably need some help in learning how to cope and perhaps gain understanding about the impact of your history. Even if one or both of you sincerely want to follow the program and make a valiant effort, it's possible that you can't do it on your own. You may need professional guidance, and at this point, a self-help book is not enough.

Additionally, all the circumstances mentioned above could benefit from support or professional help. For example, the RP will not be effective if one of you is currently experiencing major depression, serious anxiety, or traumatic loss, or has an active eating disorder, alcohol and drug addiction, or gambling problem. Also, using the RP in situations where someone has an inability to communicate, difficulty expressing compassion, or no willingness or interest in self-awareness will be difficult.

- One or both of you is bringing emotional baggage from his or her past to this relationship, and it's getting in the way of progress.

If you had a difficult upbringing or significant negative issues with an ex-partner or parent, these relationships and experiences can still affect how you feel about yourself today and how you function in the world. There will most likely be times when your current relationship and other situations will bring up those intense old feelings. If you are unwilling to recognize the impact of your previous experiences on your current functioning, this will continue to cause a significant roadblock to progress. You will probably have a difficult time giving and earning the benefit of the doubt.

- You are in the midst of a traumatic event or a crisis.

This is a tough time to absorb new and challenging information. Any learning is best achieved with a good state of mind, not a mind in crisis mode. Try to wait until the crisis or trauma subsides, if possible, before attempting to tackle the Relationship Protocol. It's important to manage life issues first.

People in crisis are usually in a heightened emotional state and, more than likely, cannot and should not try to learn new information (such as the RP) during that time. You need to have a clear mind to fully engage and participate, but you can still make an effort to be kind to each other.

Before taking on the RP, consider letting the crisis run its course, let some time pass, or wait until emotions calm down and you feel more clearheaded. Then begin by using the RP in pieces, focusing on being kind and valuing each other, or start by using only the Key Elements.

- There are serious differences between you and the other person or major problems beyond communication problems.

This is only a communication model, and it does not address specific problems beyond communication problems. The RP can show you *how* to talk about your problems, but it does not go further. Many problems can be dealt with using the RP, and if there is no resolution, then the parties agree to disagree or agree to compromise. Beyond that, the RP will not solve major differences, relationships problems, or emotional roadblocks.

If your relationship problems are only about a particular issue—not about communication at all—you may be better served seeking professional help.

No one thing is going to work for everyone

While the tenets of the Relationship Protocol are simple and straightforward, it's only a communication tool, and it's not going to be successful for everyone who uses it. Unfortunately, there is no strategy or technique that will work across the board.

If, over time, nothing seems to be changing or there's limited progress, begin by taking a look at the effort, ability, and interest level of both of you. Every relationship is different, and each person needs to assess their own willingness and ability to make changes. Use the RP to talk about your concerns and frustrations at the lack of progress.

If one of you is "talking the talk" but not "walking the walk," it may sabotage your success. If the other person is unwilling to get involved, offers minimal support, or has no interest in working on the relationship for the long term, you might want to talk to them openly and respectfully about your observations. Try to find out what is stopping them from participating fully. Use the RP to talk about how important it is for them to make an effort, and then encourage them in a positive way.

Finally, you have some other options. You may consider seeking professional help; make the determination that this is a difficult relationship and it may never change; or continue working on the relationship on your own, using the model. You can also use *The Relationship Protocol Workbook* to personalize your experience and reinforce your effort and your understanding of the RP. The choice is yours as to how to proceed. Most important, be proud of yourself for wanting to make improvements in your life.

"I still keep a copy of the RP in my wallet. Every once in a while, when I'm feeling mad or confused, I check it out, and it helps. I like having those tools literally in my back pocket."

Chapter Sixteen

ONE MORE TIME: THE RELATIONSHIP PROTOCOL MODEL

This final chapter summarizes the model and reinforces the important take-away points. The Relationship Protocol model and mantra are also at the end of the chapter for you to use as an ongoing reference.

What the Relationship Protocol can and cannot do

- The RP *cannot* fix or solve all of your problems.

THE RELATIONSHIP PROTOCOL

- The model *cannot* force anyone to change their behavior. It cannot get someone to stop spending money, change their eating habits, empty the dishwasher, or even be more considerate toward you.

- It *cannot* make a difference in your relationship if you are not committed to following the model and using it as a framework for your interactions.

- It *cannot* make you motivated to stay committed, but you must make that effort in order to be successful. If you are too casual or lazy, you will have a more difficult time.

- You *can* use your new RP communication skills to speak to the important people in your life more comfortably and without sounding negative and hurtful.

- The RP *can* be a reminder to get you back on track so things can feel good again between you and the other person.

- The model *can* help you discuss difficult topics and problems by giving you new communication tools. This is the basis of your ongoing commitment and practice.

- The RP *can* help you defuse and de-escalate during times of conflict and potential conflict.

And here's the best thing the RP model *can* do:

- In time, the Relationship Protocol can turn your communication from a pretending—"as if" you are in a healthy relationship—to a reality. You will actually have healthy communication and healthier relationships.

Make the commitment to yourself and to those closest to you.

The Relationship Protocol requires a strong commitment, self-awareness, and a desire for change. If you don't use the RP as a framework for how you think about and relate to others, the model won't work for you. Become self-reflective, and follow the Relationship Protocol for the best results.

This model is not therapy, but it's a good start

The RP can be a great strategy to help you communicate better. You're learning the foundational building blocks for communication. It can serve to clarify issues, determine where you get stuck, and perhaps point out where the relationship itself breaks down. In the end, the RP may prove to be a stepping-stone that prepares you for the work you do in therapy.

The Relationship Protocol: Core Ideas

To help you organize the information you've learned, here's a summary of the core ideas:

- Put the relationship first; make improving your relationship a priority.

- Remind each other to use the RP, learn the mantra, and stay on track.

- Don't make excuses for continuing unhealthy and hurtful behavior, because this breaks trust and will prevent your relationship from moving forward.

- Be kind, not mean or sarcastic. Know that the other person's intentions are not meant to be hurtful, because they also want to get along with you. Give each other the benefit of the doubt to build hope and trust together. Remember that you are on the same team, even during challenging times.

- Be thoughtful and respectful in your communication with *everyone*! Start with the positives and express appreciation. Think about how you want the other person to feel, and own your actions and your words.

- Changing old patterns is hard; stay with it.

An author's wish

My hope is that shortly after learning and using the model, you begin to feel more comfortable dealing with conflicts and, in general, have a better understanding of how to have healthier communication. When you are making an effort to improve your relationships, change your approach, change your response, and you can change the outcome! You can make a difference.

Most important, please remember to come back to the Relationship Protocol. It doesn't matter how long it has been since you used the model or how bad a setback you're having, the RP can be a quick refresher or a great study guide to get your relationship back on a healthy path.

I've shared my secret recipe with you: the two Key Elements and the Four Steps. Now you get to take them with you wherever you go.

The Relationship Protocol™ Model and Mantra

All close relationships can benefit from these strategies that build trust.

The two Key Elements must exist for relationships to be successful.

Key Element #1: Commitment to making your relationship better.

Key Element #2: Shift Your Thinking from what is missing or wrong with the other person or your relationship, to valuing them and having more of a relationship focus.

The Four Steps address how to communicate, build trust, and reduce emotional escalations.

Step #1: "I want to get along with you." "I want to be closer to you." And, if relevant, "I don't want to fight with you."

Step #2: "I am going to be kind. I am not going to be mean or sarcastic."

Step #3: "I am never going to do anything to intentionally hurt you." Add "from now on" if you have done hurtful things in the past.

Step #4: "I am going to give you the benefit of the doubt."

The RP Mantra: A pocket version

"I am committed to improving my relationship, and I value this person. I want to get along with them, be kind, trust their intentions, and give them the benefit of the doubt."

Notes

Notes

About the Author

D ebra M. Roberts, LCSW, is a licensed certified social worker in private practice in New York. She received her master's degree in social work from Virginia Commonwealth University. For many years, Debra worked in nonprofit organizations in the areas of mental health, poverty legal services, health, and youth programs. She has been in private practice for more than twenty years, specializing in working with adults in individual, group, and relationship therapy. Debra's communication model grew out of her extensive experience working with struggling relationships. She is also EMDRIA certified in EMDR (Eye Movement Desensitization and Reprocessing), a form of psychotherapy that helps people overcome trauma and past negative experiences. This is her first book in a planned series.

Made in the USA
San Bernardino, CA
14 November 2017